# A FIRM PLACE
# TO STAND

REVIEW COPY

# A FIRM PLACE TO STAND

*Finding Meaning in a Life with Bipolar Disorder*

## MARJA BERGEN

A FIRM PLACE TO STAND
Copyright © 2008 Marja Bergen

ISBN-10: 1-897373-45-7
ISBN-13: 978-1-897373-45-3

Scripture taken from the HOLY BIBLE, NEW INTERNATIONAL VERSION®. Copyright © 1973, 1978, 1984 International Bible Society. Used by permission of Zondervan. All rights reserved.

WORD ALIVE PRESS

Printed by Word Alive Press
131 Cordite Road, Winnipeg, MB  R3W 1S1
www.wordalivepress.ca

*I waited patiently for the Lord;*
*he turned to me and heard my cry.*
*He lifted me out of the slimy pit,*
*out of the mud and mire;*
*he set my feet on a rock*
*and gave me a firm place to stand.*
*He put a new song in my mouth,*
*a hymn of praise to our God.*
*Many will see and fear*
*and put their trust in the Lord.*

*Psalm 40:1–3*

# CONTENTS

# INTRODUCTION

I HAVE A BURNING DESIRE TO TELL YOU MY STORY. I long to tell you what I have learned from living with bipolar disorder* for four decades. I want to help others understand what it's like to have severe mental health difficulties. I want to help you, and all those who read my story, to learn from the hardships—and the joys—I have known.

When I finished my first book, *Riding the Roller Coaster: Living with Mood Disorders*, I thought I had said all I needed to say. But many things convinced me I needed to write another book, one that would testify to how God has helped me since I began searching eighteen years ago. I wrote my first book for a secular audience. This volume is for a Christian audience, for those who are struggling and for those who want to be supportive.

I've learned not to be ashamed of having bipolar disease. I feel good about who I am and don't consider myself much different from the average person, in spite of my strong moods and what they do to me at times. I know my occasional emotional difficulties are not my fault.

Medical professionals are becoming aware of the many ways a healthy spiritual life can contribute to mental well-being. Our faith can help us cope with illness of any sort. Having lived with bipolar disorder first as a non-believer and then as a follower of Christ, I know this to be true.

---

* See Appendix I for full explanation and symptoms of bipolar disorder, including depression, mania, hypomania and psychosis.

Many people need medication to keep their brains physically stable. I am one of those people. But it's my trust in a loving God that gives me a hope I can't do without. My church is a lifeline for me. I don't know what I would do without my friends there. They support me and pray for me when I'm going through rough times, times when I sometimes need to be reminded that God is still there.

When I told a friend recently that I like to be open about my battles with bipolar disorder—that I don't like to keep them secret—she said she found that unusual. She was really thinking it was weird. Yet I believe that to hide such things, or to be embarrassed about them, only serves to keep the stigma which is attached to mental illness alive. I decided many years ago that the only way to eradicate that stigma is to speak freely about it, as people do about other disorders.

I've come a long way. As a young girl I was shy and withdrawn, afraid to say much in school. Now I speak out on mental health issues. Some even call me an activist. Today I am bubbling over with a lifetime of thoughts and experiences I want to tell you about.

Bipolar disorder (also called manic depression) is a difficult diagnosis to accept, but a rich and productive life is possible, much more so today than in the past. If you have been diagnosed with bipolar disorder, I hope this book will encourage you, with the help of God, to find a better life for yourself.

# PART ONE:
## BIPOLAR DISORDER

*Chapter 1*

# LIVING WITH BIPOLAR DISORDER

## The Beginning

THE FIRST TIME I knew I was sick, I was nineteen. Psychosis had taken over my life before anyone, including me, knew what was happening.

I was a second-year student at the brand new Simon Fraser University near Vancouver, British Columbia. During the opening ceremonies, my senses were overwhelmed by the dazzling silver of the fresh concrete slabs that made up the modern architecture. I felt dizzy; everything seemed unreal. I struggled to stay connected with what was happening around me, but it was as if I were in a dream world, disconnected. Looking back now, I know that my problems had already started—at the beginning of that school year.

In the university bookstore, I bought books on every subject, books I couldn't afford and didn't need for my courses. Philosophy and religion books especially fascinated me. I read bits and pieces, but was not able to concentrate long enough to read anything through. My thoughts traveled rapidly and endlessly. I felt I had discovered the reason for everything, as though I comprehended the universe and the mysteries of how everything worked. I felt I could see how science and religion fit together.

When I was with friends, I expounded on deep philosophical ideas, speaking ever faster until they could no longer make sense of what I was saying. My words could not keep up with my fast-moving mind. The endless overflow of thoughts would not stop. I was convinced that articles I read in the newspaper and programs I heard on the radio contained messages specifically meant for me, even when they were in a foreign language.

After a while though, deep down, I began to suspect there was something wrong. I remember an occasion when I was in the cafeteria with some others and we heard the sirens of an emergency vehicle. Under my breath I began to sing a song popular at the time, "They're coming to take me away, aha. They're coming to take me away." I was only half joking.

I lived through a terrifying sequence of psychotic thoughts and imagined experiences. In November, I was admitted to Crease Clinic, part of Essondale, British Columbia's large psychiatric institution. Over the next year and a half, I spent a total of nine months there, thought to be and treated as, a patient with schizophrenia. It was not until twenty-five years later that I received the diagnosis of bipolar 1 disorder.

## My Roller Coaster Ride

I'M ONE OF those individuals who despises roller coasters and all amusement park rides. I don't enjoy the excitement of being dropped from steep heights, tossed violently around corners and then, after a slow steep climb, falling again screaming into what seems like a deep abyss. I don't like the idea of being strapped in, with no escape. Give me the security of solid ground. There's nothing more wonderful to me than stable earth beneath my feet.

It doesn't seem right then that I, of all people, should be forced onto this roller coaster ride of the mind. During my episodes, there's no escaping the dramatic moods that take me high and low.

All too often during the past forty years, I've experienced the euphoria and high energy of mania. My mind becomes over-active and ideas tumble out in quick succession as I speak and write. I jump from one topic to another. What I read becomes extraordinarily clear and I seem to find a deeper understanding of philosophical truths. At times like these, I feel as though I can do everything and I take on more projects and responsibilities than I can handle. In social situations my personality becomes effervescent.

Other times I drop into depression. My entire being becomes sluggish and the activities I usually enjoy don't interest me. Socially I withdraw and I find nothing to talk about. I see the world as a colorless place and life as unbearably painful. Eventually it becomes difficult to move from my bed.

Sometimes, in the midst of these highs and lows, I wish I could get off the ride. Even the manic phase stops being fun. There comes a point when I wish I could end the constant racing from activity to activity. The flood of ideas that keep my mind so busy exhausts me. I long for peace; I long for a good night's sleep. Gradually I do recover and I'm able to slow down and rest. Such relief that is! Often, however, this respite is short-lived. Before long and without warning I find myself trapped in lethargy.

Fortunately these extremes come only in the form of episodes. Usually my moods are halfway between the highs and lows and I feel and function as normally as the average person. Most of the time, I have my feet in a secure place—exactly where I like them.

# I Am the Clay

*"And yet, Lord, you are our Father. We are the clay, and you are the potter. We are formed by your hand." (Isaiah 64:8)*

I'M NOT SORRY for myself, though I may sound it at times. These moods are difficult to bear and I do everything I can to avoid them, but in general, life is good. I must live with this disorder and I've learned to accept it. I am not angry at God for having made me this way. I would not be who I am without it. Every episode has had an impact on me. Every time I recover, I find I've learned a little more about life. My faith grows. Each time, it's as though I go through a fire, am tested and survive—a stronger person than before.

Suffering has taught me compassion. It has helped me want to help others cope with their pain. I love the challenge of creating inspirational booklets and other materials for people in hospitals and care facilities because I know what it is like to be institutionalized and lonely. I know the feelings these people deal with and I try to supply them with reading that will comfort them.

Helping to remove the stigma attached to mental illness has become very important for me. I have long tried to help others understand mental illness so that those who suffer as I do will receive better support and care. This gives me a clear purpose in life, something to work towards—something to get up for in the morning.

My extreme moods have given me a sensitivity that has helped me become an accomplished photographer. Through the portraits I make of children and nature, I express my feelings. Because my feelings are strong, my pictures become strong.

At times of depression and mania, passages from the Bible have held more intense meaning for me than they ever could have if my mood had been normal. I know that the clarity of understanding I experience is not simply an "insane response," but a heightened awareness, one I value, one that helps me grow.

My health is not something I can take for granted. For this reason I try to make every day of wellness count for something. I feel rich. I feel grateful for the full, active life I'm able to lead. My road is tough at times, but it has taken me in directions I had never imagined possible.

Though I have often become ill and unable to function as I thought I should, my disorder does have value too. Perhaps God intended some of us to be different in this way. Biographies have shown that numerous writers, artists and musicians probably had bipolar disorder. In Chapter 10 I've written about famous people and how they were affected by intense mood swings.

Without my severe mood swings would I have the inspiration to do the work that means so much to me? I'm quite sure I wouldn't. I do believe the great Potter, had a reason for making me this way.

# A Time of Depression

DEPRESSION CAN COME upon me at any time. Yet, when all is well—when I'm stable or a little high—I don't in my heart believe it possible. At times I feel invincible. When my mood begins to dip, I tend to tell myself it's just a little glitch and I'll recover within days.

Then, when I'm down, I can't see my way out. I'm in the proverbial tunnel with no light at the end. I feel lethargic, often without the energy to move off my bed. Everything slows down: my thinking, moving and speaking. Work becomes difficult—at times impossible. Even the hobbies I love hold no interest for me. Sometimes I get very sad and feel useless. Life seems pointless. The following is what I journaled during such a time:

I'm tired and, over the last three days, I've felt a persistent darkness. My depressions often start this way: At first my body feels weary, but I'm comfortably contemplative—quiet. It is as though I dip into a deep well in search of clear refreshing water to drink. But before I can get to it, something grabs me and holds me suspended. I can't reach down to the water to have a swallow or up to the air to breathe. It's as though I'm paralyzed.

Everything had been going well for me. I have the church, friends and family who love me, rewarding projects. I'm grateful, but at times like this, I'm too weak to bear the weight of all these treasures. Good things have almost as much weight as bad things.

I feel an utter loss of purpose. I see no reason for being. Maybe it's this loss that makes me feel so distant from God.

I drag myself around, trying hard to do the things I need to do. But how can I get all the sludge out of my heart, that stuff that makes me feel so heavy and sad? I have ugly feelings about everything in my life and in the world. My entire being is a big yawn. I wish I could have a good cry.

It's easy to say "trust in God" or "don't be afraid." But when I'm truly depressed, I can't reach God. I believe God's love exists is real, yet God is so intangible. It's hard to truly feel that love. I feel distanced from God—abandoned. I ask my closest friends to pray for me—to pray that the depression will lift. There's comfort in knowing that they care enough to remember me in their prayers.

# Nothing Helped

*"I am confined and cannot escape." (Psalm 88:8b)*

SOME YEARS AGO my husband Wes and I did something I had dreamed about for many years. We rented a beachfront cabin on one of British Columbia's Gulf Islands. We're not rich. This was not something we could easily afford. But we hoped that a week relaxing in such a beautiful spot might help rid me of the blackness that had shrouded my entire being for so long.

The cabin was not exactly rustic. It was more like a luxurious house. At the back was a piece of lawn, furnished with a couple of lounge chairs. Three steps down from the lawn was the beach, complete with tide pools to explore. From inside, a huge window overlooked the water and gave us a view of a tiny island, close to shore. It was inhabited by a family of sea lions. We could hear their barking as they sunned themselves on the rocks.

We could not have dreamed of a more idyllic setting. Yet my misery remained. Nothing could budge me from the depths. I tried hard to enjoy myself, but felt trapped in a lonely, dark world. For me, the sun and the waves were covered in plastic wrapping. I could not feel, hear, or see the world as it was to others. Grass and flowers all appeared gray.

When I'm in the midst of depression like this, it's almost impossible to see beyond the moment. I can't believe it could ever be possible to climb out of the gloom that envelops me. It's difficult to imagine I ever felt good in the past—or to believe that those good feelings were ever genuine.

This period of my life was one of the darkest I can remember. Escaping it took months of effort and much trial and error with medication. But when a better mood did surface, the world became a new place. Colors were vivid once more and I felt I could once again grab hold of real life. The contrast was remarkable! David knew this feeling and wrote about it in Psalm 30:11. He prayed, *"You turned my wailing into dancing; you removed my sackcloth and clothed me with joy."*

## Stress

BIPOLAR DISORDER IS not a clinical problem that simply pops up in my life now and then. While I need medication, self care and support to manage my health, these do not always halt the onset of symptoms. Stress plays a big role in my illness.

Stress causes health problems for individuals with all kinds of medical conditions. Many illnesses can be triggered or made worse by an unusual amount stress. The same holds true for mental health problems.

Many times my highs and lows are brought on by situations beyond my control. I can't always avoid stress. My mother and mother-in-law need care; Christmas traditions need to be lived up to; my son gets married. Sometimes a physical problem crops up to make my life difficult.

I tend to take on a lot of responsibility. I can't help it. When a friend is struggling, I might take her a jar of soup. When a sister needs support, I'm there, even if it's only by telephone. I often co-ordinate family gatherings. When I'm asked to talk on photography or mood disorders, I can't say no. I take on big responsibilities as well. Writing this book was one of them, one I felt driven to complete.

Perhaps part of the reason I take on so much is my frequent hypomanic disposition. Or perhaps it's my personality. I suspect it's a little of each.

I try hard to keep things in balance; I try hard not to take on more than I can handle. But unforeseen needs appear at every turn. Countless times I have suddenly found myself swamped and I lose control. I try to shed some of the work but find that most of it, the important responsibilities, is still there. I try to find others to take on some of it, but ever so often there is no one willing or able to take over.

Sometimes during such stress, I have done things or said things I've later been sorry for, so sorry that my mood has blackened. I've hurt people and then feared that the damage might be irreparable. I hide under the warmth of a thick blanket and curl up, wishing for sleep, wishing that time would pass and that the darkness would give way to light. "Please, God," I pray, "work quickly to heal the pain within myself and the one I hurt. Don't let the wounds fester. Forgive me, Lord, for I didn't know what I was do-ing. Give me the courage to call those I have hurt so I can let them know I am sorry."

I find comfort in Psalm 34:18: *"The Lord is close to the bro-kenhearted and saves those who are crushed in spirit."*

Excessive stress often means that I need to adjust my medica-tion. Sometimes I simply need to rest and withdraw from my busy schedule and give myself time to recover. When I do that, I feel shame and somewhat defeated. I hate letting down the people who depend on me.

# A Time of Mania

MANIA IS THE opposite of depression. My energy rises, my thoughts speed up and my mind floods with ideas and plans. I'm high and I feel capable of anything. But I am also prone to poor judgment which can get me into severe trouble. I wrote the following in my journal at such a time:

Wes has been gone for a week and I'm beginning to suffer. I feel lonely and Jeff, my son, is seldom home. The worst of it is that I'm beginning to feel as if I'm on a treadmill—coming up with one creative idea after another, trying to execute them all at once. It makes me dizzy, but I can't stop. I feel as though I don't have any time to lose. As long as I'm well, I want to—no, I must—be productive. There's so much I want to do!

When Wes is home, this is not as much of a problem. He holds me back—in a good way. He comes home and I stop working, we visit and I cook dinner. There's no chance of my getting lost, trying to follow a dozen tangents at once. If I become unreasonable, he tells me so and I listen (though not always).

At six o'clock tonight, I realized that all I'd eaten today was a bowl of All-Bran and a large side of fries. I'd also had lots of coffee.

I've been writing a fair amount too. I think it's good that I've only sent letters to Dr. Panikkar and Dr. McDougall. I almost sent one to Rev. Dale, but held back—better play it safe. I also wrote a thank you card to Tom for the photograph he gave me, but I'm a bit worried that I went overboard in my praise of his work.

That's one of my worst problems. I so often lack good judgment, especially when I'm not stable, which is quite often. What would I do without Wes? Wonderful, patient and understanding Wes!

# Dancing as Fast as I Can

I HAD BEEN somewhat manic for several weeks. My life had been full of activity—too full. I'd been writing, doing photography jobs, looking after the needs of my mother and mother-in-law (each of them an hour's drive away), trying to run my household, spending time with friends. And then Christmas came upon me, with the huge effort that entails. If that weren't enough, we were planning a big trip immediately after Christmas.

With the help of an extra sedative, I managed. I was once again able to focus on one thing at a time. I slept the usual seven hours each night and was able to take my usual twenty-minute cat-nap in the afternoon.

Yet it became more and more difficult to cope with the many assorted tasks that filled my days. I was able to focus on one at a time as I needed to. However, the constantly changing gears were beginning to exhaust me. My mind felt dizzy whenever I moved from one activity to another.

As I stood at the gas station to fill my car, I was overwhelmed by the busyness of the world around me: the roar of the cars as they sped by on the busy street and the strip mall across the way, overflowing with more products than could ever be sold.

I felt that the world had spun out of control, with everyone in it sucked into the worship of excess. In studying the people I met, I vividly saw how stressed out they were. This is what loss of child-hood is all about, I thought. This is the loss of innocence and pu-rity. The quiet life gone forever. I longed for a simpler era. I longed for the days before television, computers and cars. I wanted out of the confusion; I wanted peace.

With Christmas season in full swing, flyers made our newspa-pers bulge. I came to despise them and wasted no time tossing them into the recycling bin. What a waste of trees!

The world was moving at far too fast a pace. I could relate to the title of the movie, "I'm Dancing as Fast as I can." I felt I was

12

racing; I felt out of breath. Yet I didn't know how to stop. I had to keep going. There was so much to do!

It was in this state that I saw Dr. Long. His diagnosis: "Your hypomania is beginning to get out of hand. We need to increase your dose of antipsychotic medication. With that you should be as good as new." I sighed and sputtered, "But it's my workload that's causing the problem. What I need is more support, not another pill!"

# A Period of Mixed Moods

*"If I go up to the heavens, you are there; if I make my bed in the depths, you are there." (Psalm 139:8)*

THE LAST STRAW—the final thing that started my mind working overtime and threw me into a dangerous mood disturbance—was my renewed recognition of the need to build mental health awareness. This had been a strong interest of mine for many years. I had taken on the job of promoting the annual mental health retreat, presented by the Mennonite Central Committee Supportive Care Services in Abbotsford, British Columbia. To do a truly good job of encouraging attendance, church leaders' support in particular, I knew I had to address some wider issues. I would need to draw attention to the importance of spirituality to mental health. I would need to help Christian congregations understand why it is so important to support those with mental health problems, especially within their own church families. I began to draw up big plans for a media campaign—manic-sized plans. A hypomanic mood quickly developed.

Many of my manic-depressive episodes follow stressful events coming together. My last episode before I began writing this book came about during a period of pressure in my life. There was only a single negative stressor—worry about my aging mother and mother-in-law, both in their nineties. The other stressors were all activities I found enjoyable and exciting: the busyness of Christmas, which included hosting several social gatherings; a part-time photography business; enthusiasm about the publicity work I was beginning for the retreat. The excitement created problems. Good stress can harm one's health as much as bad.

During this time I read books, heard stories and spoke to people—all showing me that mental health issues are still poorly understood, even in this modern day. This impressed on me, more strongly than ever, the need for education about mental health issues.

My emotions became intense. I was tossed between concern at the ignorance I witnessed and anger at the unfairness of the lack of support for those in need. I knew what I had to do, yet at the same time I feared the task before me. Nevertheless, I was determined to make a difference.

Storms raged within me. I wrote emails to my pastor, pouring out my hopes and frustrations, peppering him with questions. In the process, and out of great need, I drew closer to God.

Once more, I found myself on a roller coaster ride of strong feelings and over-stimulation. What followed was a two and a half month episode where mildly high moods alternated with brief periods of depression, a condition referred to as a mixed state.

There were many days when I went from elated hyperactivity to sadness or anxiety. Often the nights consumed me with depression. In the morning this would lift abruptly as I met people in the mall, at the gym, or at church. My elated mood would once again take over.

At other times I felt gloom in the middle of the day, sandwiched between hours of hectic creativity. I couldn't predict when I would be up or down. Interestingly, while I was with people, I always felt happy and outgoing—a blessing. I don't think most people were aware of what I was going through.

Most mornings I spent as much as two hours in meditation and prayer, reading and writing. My Bible became more precious to me than ever. I searched it, prayerfully looking for verses that would help me deal with my feelings and thoughts. God didn't let me down, speaking to me through the Word and helping me weather the storms. One verse I hung onto during this period was Zephaniah 3:17. *"The Lord your God is with you...he will quiet you with his love."* Repeating that promise comforted me and slowed me down when my mind raced.

Amazing how faith in God and belief in his Word can provide such precious comfort and encouragement when we need it most! I would never abandon the pills my doctor prescribes. I know I need them for the biochemical treatment of my disorder. But when things get tough, God's Word is the best medication of all. It heals my soul.

This was a difficult period, but much good came of it. I've once more become determined, as I was when I wrote my first book, *Riding the Roller Coaster*, to give everything I can to help people understand the needs of those with mental disorders.

Though the retreat was still six months away, I was driven to begin work immediately. I wrote letters and articles and talked to those who needed to be informed. I also began writing this book. My feelings were strong; I was inspired. It was a struggle to harness my moods and retain day-to-day control. Yet, the most important thing to me, the publicity work, came easily. I focused well and the issues were clear in my mind.

As I write this, my mood has settled back to normal. My mind works more slowly. Words are more difficult to find. I have to work harder to craft my letters, articles and these pages. But thankfully, though my enthusiasm is still strong, life is more manageable now. God has helped me safely through and I'm at peace once more.

## Recovery After Five Weeks of Instability

*"He lifted me out of the slimy pit, out of the mud and mire; he set my feet on a rock and gave me a firm place to stand. He put a new song in my mouth." (Psalm 40:2–3)*

15

~

*Such a relief!...no longer to be caught in a web of deep thought and emotions...no longer to sit for two or more hours at a time, my mind working so hard I become distant from the real world. Such a relief to rise to the surface and to be able to think and function with my feet in a firm place again! Such a relief not to feel so deeply that my joy becomes unbearable!*

*Thank you, God, for helping me return, for helping me to find solid ground once more. Thank you for the fresh energy, for the ability to carry out what I want to do. Thank you for staying with me on the journey and for helping me to keep my hand in yours.*

I DON'T KNOW if what I went through could be defined as a series of highs and lows. The lows came to me only once in a while. They were more feelings of doom than depression. What might be considered high was simply a feeling of great joy, but often so overpowering it was difficult to contain. The most debilitating part of these weeks was the thinking that consumed me and kept me in a fog. During those times I found it difficult to move my mind and my body. Even when I wasn't in deep thought, this fogginess would not go away.

After coming off a roller coaster ride like this, I feel great relief and peace. I'm in touch with the world around me again. Following great struggles, I am transformed and renewed.

Such an ordeal seems to me like a time of testing. It forces me to sift through what I want to bring to my life. It gives me a clearer picture of what is most important and where God truly wants me to go. I gain a renewed sense of purpose. Today I'm fully ready and eager to carry on with the work God has given me.

# Psychosis

THE 2001 MOVIE, *A Beautiful Mind,* is a true story of psychosis. It follows the life of John Nash, a brilliant mathematician, as he becomes delusional and, in his deranged mind, is involved in a terrifying conspiracy plot. Along with him, and without realizing it, the audience is sucked into an ever-escalating loss of touch with reality. Viewers learn exactly what it feels like to live with the nightmares of delusions and hallucinations a person with schizophrenia experiences.

Psychosis can be part of bipolar type 1 disorder. It can come about from untreated depression or mania. This was true for me. My last psychotic episodes are in the distant past now, but memories of them are firmly fixed in my mind, especially those I had when I was nineteen.

Most people have a difficult time grasping the meaning of "psychosis."* One victim described the beginning of psychosis this way: "...much of the seeming deterioration of communication is due more to the limitation of vocabulary and language, and less due to a basic error in the thought processes." That has been my experience as well. Expressing the flood of thoughts that fills my mind is like having an exciting story to write, running out of paper, but still carrying on. I'm not able to contain all that's inside me: the thoughts, joys, or pains. My mind overflows. In the words of yet another who has experienced it: "Psychosis is the brain's way of coping with overload."

# Paranoia

PARANOIA, ONE FORM of psychosis, is one of the ugliest parts of the illness. When I was paranoid I felt as though someone was plotting against me, usually some imagined power. But sometimes

---

* See Appendix I for descriptions of various types of psychosis.

I feared real people, mistrusting those around me, even family members.

When I was four months pregnant, Wes and I moved into our first house, a particularly stressful experience for me. The adjustment of living in the spaciousness of a two-level house, rather than a one-bedroom apartment, was not easy. Worse, my doctor had taken me off my medication to prevent possible harm to my baby. I was not in good emotional shape.

One day, after bringing the laundry in off the clothes line, I discovered some facecloths missing. I became extremely distressed. Not in my right mind, I began to suspect that our new neighbors had stolen them. In my confused state, I was not able to do a good job of looking for them. I worried for days and, in the process, developed a huge mistrust of our new neighbors. A short time later, I found them. I felt relieved...and stupid. I had lost them because of my disorganized state of mind and because I had not yet adjusted to the abundance of new closet and cupboard space.

Years later, during another episode, a number of things tumbled out of the freezer compartment of the refrigerator as I opened it. Suspicions haunted me that my son had orchestrated this in an effort to drive me mad. My son is not the kind of person to play tricks like that and he loves me too much to do me harm. Later I felt ashamed for having harbored such unreasonable suspicions.

Paranoia must be one of the worst things I've experienced with this disorder. It frightens me to think that my mind can become so unreasonably mistrustful. How can I come to think such terrible things about the people I love? Yet, when it happens, these thoughts are beyond my ability to control; they become my reality.

*Chapter 2*

# RECEIVING TREATMENT

## Misdiagnosis

I SPENT A three-month period at Crease Clinic beginning in 1965. When I was discharged, I did reasonably well for seven months, even working at an office job. But psychosis returned, and I was again admitted. This time I stayed for six interminable months.

Throughout my hospital stay, my doctors believed I had schizophrenia, a diagnosis which stayed with me for at least twenty-five years. Only in 1995 did my doctor at the time diagnose my disorder as Bipolar Type 1 and start me on a mood stabilizer. Because of the psychotic element in my condition, I remained on an antipsychotic medication as well.

Although my records showed that I had schizophrenia, my doctor in the sixties did not tell me the nature of my disease, and I never asked. I naively assumed that my illness was unique to me. I did not think there might be a name for it. It didn't occur to me there could be many other people in the world who suffered in the same way I did.

I first began to suspect my diagnosis sometime in the early eighties when I read a story about a violent murder by a man with bipolar disorder (in those days referred to as "manic depression"). The newspaper article included a description of the symptoms, much like the lists I've included in the appendix of this book, and I recognized they were the same symptoms I had. Although violence was a potential part of this man's make-up, thankfully this was not something I was troubled with.

Although I believed I was bipolar, a doctor I began seeing in 1985 obtained my hospital records and upheld the opinion that I had schizophrenia. I quietly suspected it wrong.

In this day and age, patients should be aware of their diagnosis, no matter how difficult it may be to live with. While we might wish that doctors would educate every patient, the truth is they don't have time. We need to do the research ourselves. Helpful information is widely available in libraries and on the internet. Support organizations exist for almost every known disease. Gone are the days when we relied on our doctors for everything we required for our treatment. All the health issues I've encountered have taught me that I need to do everything I can to educate myself. I want to ensure that I'm treated as well as possible.

I suspect, though, that in my case—in the sixties and seventies—not receiving a label was helpful to me. At that time, the prognosis for people with schizophrenia was not good. If my disorder had been named, and incorrectly at that, would I have survived the way I did? Or might I have assumed there was no hope? Would I have worked as hard as I did to return to full functioning?

I believe now that being in the dark for so many years was a blessing. I am sure that God has had reasons for all the turns in my life, and I am content that all has worked out for the best. There's no point in crying today about the wrong diagnosis or wrong medications I received yesterday. I try to live as the apostle Paul did: *"Forgetting what is behind and straining toward what is ahead..."* (Philippians 3:13b)

# Recognizing Symptoms

ONCE DEPRESSION OR mania has taken hold, the symptoms are simple enough to identify. But it would be better if we could see them in the beginning stages, before we're into a full-blown episode. Yet these symptoms often appear almost unnoticeably. My husband, Wes, is usually the first to see when things aren't right with me. When he does, and when he finds it necessary, he gently points out his concerns and suggests I look into further treatment.

Unfortunately, when I'm in a manic or hypomanic state, he has difficulty convincing me that there's anything to worry about. I enjoy the elation. I can't believe that the optimism I feel and my ability to accomplish so much means that I'm sick. Socially I feel freer. My conversation is more vibrant, and my thoughts are well-focused. I feel sharp—more intelligent than ever. How could anything that feels so right be wrong? This is who I'm really meant to be. I couldn't be more well...and I don't want to let go. When I'm in such an up mood, convincing me that I need pills to take all this away is difficult.

Sometimes I'm fortunate, and I'm more able to see myself as others see me. At times I notice how everyone around me—friends, store clerks, everyone I meet—seems subdued, even sad. It's a strange thing to become aware of this contrast between others' moods and mine. I wonder why these people are not laughing more, why they're so serious about everything. When I become conscious of this, I know that I need to settle down. I try to take a break from people, busy activity and anything that stimulates me too much. This self-awareness is sometimes possible, especially today, now that I'm older and understand my disorder better.

Yet most of the time, I struggle to understand that I need to seek help. The nature of this disorder makes listening to reason difficult, especially when I'm high. Though I have lived with this disorder for forty years, I still have trouble. Thank God for a husband who is patient with me!

# A Treatable Disorder

BIPOLAR DISORDER WILL be with me all my life. Highs and lows will repeat themselves many times. I need to take advantage of the treatment that's available. If I don't, my functioning will be severely impaired.

I will always have to take medications, and I must take them regularly. If I don't, I may go into a depression. Or, worse, I may go into a manic episode in which I could lose a lot. Many people with bipolar disorder have lost their reputations when they've gone into an uncontrollable high. They've lost friends because of unacceptable, erratic behavior. Even relationships with spouses can suffer. Marriages often don't survive the turmoil. And suicide is always a threat. Even I, an optimistic person who loves and embraces life, have had periods when I would like to die.

This all sounds very bad, yet I feel confident about my future. Today, bipolar disorder is one of the most treatable of mental illnesses. There are numerous medications that make a close-to-normal life possible. My medications help to stabilize my moods and reduce the number of episodes I have. When depression and mania do occur, they are less severe than they would otherwise be. In fact, in recent years mania has not been a problem for me. When I become high, it has only been a low high, or hypomania.

# Medications

IN THE RECENT past, I've taken mainly two kinds of medication. One is a mood stabilizer to control my mood swings. The other is an antipsychotic medication because I have Bipolar Type I, which includes problems with psychosis. When I become depressed, I take an anti-depressant. But I have to be careful with anti-depressants and can't stay on them for extended periods. Anti-depressants carry the risk of pushing people with my form of bipolar into mania.

Sometimes my treatment loses its effectiveness, and symptoms develop. Then my doctor and I need to put our heads together and decide on a different dosage or search for an alternate kind of medication. A period of trial and error follows as we try to find what works best for me.

# Learning to Do What I'm Told

IN 1965, WHEN I first became sick, psychiatric medications were in their infancy. Lithium, the first mood stabilizer, had come into use only a decade earlier. Despite the long history of bipolar disorder, effective treatment has only been around since the 1950s. Since then, scientists have developed many other drugs to help people cope with manic depression, as well as other mental illnesses. If this were 1940, I would probably not be leading the full life I now have. I would not be sitting here writing this book.

However, during my first eight years with the disorder, I did not understand the importance of taking my medications on a regular basis. I did not realize that my condition was chronic. I fully expected to recover. Taking pills indefinitely was an idea I had to adjust to. Like so many newly diagnosed individuals, I had a hard time learning to follow doctor's orders.

Every time I started feeling better, I thought I was cured for good and would stop taking the pills. Soon after, my symptoms would invariably return. Looking back, I am amazed at how long it took me to understand how vital medications are to the chemical balance I need. Eventually, after many trials, I did learn. Now I take my medications "religiously."

Several times, acquaintances tried to talk me out of taking my medication, suggesting that counseling, faith or health food supplements could help me overcome my illness. I am intensely offended when my illness is made light of in this way. These people had no idea how devastating my symptoms could be. They had no idea what they were playing with—a dysfunction of my brain. Would they tell people with diabetes to throw away their insulin?

Some Christians believe treatments such as these are not God's way of dealing with emotional difficulties. But I believe the researchers who develop the drugs that have become important in all areas of health are part of God's provision, empowered by God to work for our well-being. Thanks to modern research, doctors can now better deal with mental illnesses, in the same way they are better able to deal with cancer, heart disease and the many other health problems we face.

I am fortunate to have a psychiatrist I trust, someone who keeps up to date with medical advances. With the constant improvement of medications and my doctor's increased understanding of how to use them, my life has improved significantly since the early years of my illness. I have fewer episodes than in past years. Even two years ago, a new drug I started taking allowed me to function at a level I had never experienced before.

Modern medicine has made it possible for me to be a complete, contributing member of my community. I am grateful for this and hope I never take it for granted.

# Psychotherapy

MY PSYCHIATRIST IS a medical doctor who, unlike psychologists or counselors, can prescribe medication for patients with mental disorders. I visit my psychiatrist on a regular basis. When I am stable, I go about every three months. When I have problems, I go more often. Each time we assess whether I have symptoms we need to deal with. Sometimes my dosage needs correcting. Sometimes I need to change to another medication.

Having a psychiatrist with whom I can discuss problems on a regular basis is an important part of my treatment. Life with manic depression is difficult. I have many issues to cope with. A professional can help me sort through the inevitable problems with stress, self-esteem, interpersonal relations and work. Relapse becomes less likely.

Unfortunately, many of today's psychiatrists have never been trained in counseling. I have found that having a counselor available when my doctor isn't able to deal sufficiently with my deeper emotional issues is invaluable. My counselor is a Christian and is able to address my spiritual as well as my psychological needs.

## A Safe Haven

VISITS WITH MY psychiatrist, Dr. Long, are times I look forward to. I feel relaxed and at home in his office. Here I am free to talk about anything that may have been bothering me, problems that have come up or questions about my medications. I can discuss symptoms and know he will treat me with respect and without judgment. I enjoy telling him about all that is new in my life. He is like a friend to me.

Dr. Long usually begins the 45-minute session by asking me how life has been since I last saw him. His questions might include:

- How many hours have you been sleeping at night?
- How much exercise are you getting?
- Have you had any problems with memory?
- Have you spent time with friends?
- What activities have you been engaged in?

If I've been having problems with my moods, he might ask whether my mind has been over-active or how my concentration level is. He often asks me whether I'm keeping up with my housekeeping, a question that quite honestly annoys me. I secretly wonder whether he asks the same question of his male patients. But I understand why he asks. Being disorganized is a strong indication of depression or mania.

Although Dr. Long is not a Christian, he is more than willing to let me talk to him about spiritual matters. Because my faith greatly influences my day-to-day life and moods, such topics often come up. He is interested in my beliefs, and we have, on several occasions, referred to a Bible he keeps on his shelf. To have a doctor who respects my spiritual needs and understands how important they are to me is a gift; I count myself fortunate.

My doctor is an important partner in my effort to stay well. For a number of years in the seventies, I didn't have a psychiatrist. No one helped me when my mood swings approached dangerous levels. I didn't feel safe and had recurring nightmares about becoming psychotic and not being able to find help. My general practitioner renewed my medications, but he wasn't well versed in this area of medicine and didn't adjust dosages at times when it would have been helpful. We never discussed my mental health. Of course, in those days knowledge of psychiatry was not as advanced as it is today. Today many primary care physicians are familiar with the basic treatments for emotional problems.

My psychiatrist has become well acquainted with me and my problems and knows what medicines are best for my condition. I feel confident that the biochemical part of my care is being well looked after. Having a specialist who keeps up with the rapidly changing world of psychiatric medicine gives me a sense of security.

## A Treatment That Finally Worked

BACK IN THE sixties, during my second session at Crease Clinic— the period that lasted six months—my condition was poor. Even months after my admission, I had failed to improve. I was severely depressed and seldom spoke. There was little going on in my head, so I had nothing to talk about. I can still remember the boredom. Mealtimes were the most interesting part of my day—not that the meals served at the institution were particularly good, it's just that food was the only pleasure left to me. I ate well and, with the help of my daily dose of chloral hydrate, slept well. I gained a lot of weight.

My hospital records for that period show that I was over-medicated. This was not unusual for this time in history. Psychiatric medicine was still in its infancy, and medications were sometimes used inappropriately. My mouth hung open much of the time. I walked around in a daze, not totally conscious of what was going on around me. I slept through several emergencies, including one when a patient set her mattress on fire while smoking in bed.

Today I wonder how much of my failure to recover was due to this stupor. All I could do was watch what happened around me. How can a person become well when her ability to join in the life around her is taken away?

Four and a half months after my second admission to hospital, with no significant improvement, the doctor finally reduced my medications and gave me six electro-convulsive shock treatments (ECT). Within six weeks of beginning these treatments, I improved dramatically and was discharged, finally ready to live again.

ECT worked for me. However, I'm convinced that simply treating me with less medication from the beginning might have helped me recover faster. I can't comprehend how a medical professional could judge a patient's functioning when that patient is so heavily drugged! ECT might not have been necessary at all.

But we can't judge present-day mental health care by the standards of the sixties.* Today's medications are more effective, and doctors are more knowledgeable about using them. The ECT I received was a significantly cruder form than what is used today; there was a danger of long-term damage. Now, ECT is only used when medications have been tried without success and the danger of suicide is extreme.

---

* See Appendix I for description of ECT in the 21st century.

# An Attitude of Hope

I'VE LEARNED THAT the best way to accept treatment, no matter how sick I might be, is with an attitude of hope. Once I have a doctor I respect, I must trust the medications he prescribes. I've witnessed fellow patients in hospital who were afraid of the medications and refused to take them. They lived with fear, a fear that took over in other areas of their lives as well. Recovery was difficult for them. Fear aggravated their problems and made them sicker.

Many people fear psychiatric medications because of stories from the past, when there was less knowledge and medications were often abused by doctors who did not know better. These people often try to improve on their own, coping on their own terms, often resorting to alcohol or street drugs. Addictions become a problem for many.

Most responsible doctors today do not prescribe drugs that will cause addiction or make us walk around like zombies. They monitor side-effects and will change our medications if they become problematic. Today's medications are the best we've ever had. The first ones we try may not be right for us, but we must give them a chance. If one doesn't work, or if we have an adverse reaction, we try another, with hope intact.

I've found that the confidence I bring to my treatment has a lot to do with how effective that treatment will be. If I can use the medications my doctor prescribes, believing in my own ability to be well, I cope much better. I've learned that fear can be crippling, while trust is healing.

It takes an attitude of trust towards my earthly physician and my heavenly Father to help me relax and cope with symptoms when they arise. God is ultimately the overseer, the One who has made modern psychiatry possible. I've learned that if I can trust God, I don't need to fear anything. *"In God, whose word I praise, in God I trust; I will not be afraid. What can mortal man do to me?"* (Psalm 56:4)

# PART TWO:
## GROWING

*Chapter 3*

# From CHILDHOOD
# to MOTHERHOOD

## Childhood

LINED UP WITH the other children, stark naked, I fearfully waited my turn. The steamy room echoed with the shouting of nurses as they shoved us under the shower, one at a time. I had the first shower of my life there. Not accustomed to any more water than I had seen in our small washtub at home, I was terrified of standing under the hot cascade, frightened of it splashing all over my face.

It was 1953 in Holland. I was seven years old and spending the first of three annual six-week periods away from home. The government sponsored me, along with many other city kids, to go to the countryside for my health. The first two years, I went to a facility for children who were thought to need a cleaner environment and more nutritious meals. It was referred to as a "colony." Parents were only allowed to visit for one afternoon, half-way through our time there.

Traumatic memories remain with me to this day. By nature I was a quiet and shy girl, and I don't remember making any friends in these homes, or even saying very much.

As we lay in our rows of beds in the dorm at night, a nurse came in at lights-out-time and ordered us all to face the same direction. This was to help settle us down and keep us from talking. My desire to turn over was unbearable, and sleep did not come easily.

I'm sure my negative recollections might have been colored by the misery and loneliness I felt. Other children there might not have had such unpleasant memories. But it didn't seem to me there was much kindness in those homes.

I remember a contest that ran for the full six weeks I spent at one of the colonies, to see who could eat the most slices of bread. Fortunately it was brown bread they fed us rather than the white variety I got at home. Dinners were more interesting, frequently including a tasty ragout.

I had some happier recollections. One came, oddly enough, as the result of a terrifying occasion when I accidentally became locked in a washroom. Everyone went out for a walk, while I was left behind. I cried and screamed, afraid of not being found. A sympathetic nurse rescued me, gently calmed me down and set me at a table by the window with coloring pencils and paper. Here, alone in that bright and quiet corner, I had the most wonderful time.

Although most of my time there was traumatic, I enjoyed the time we made a giant wall hanging, a gift for Queen Juliana, whose summer palace was nearby. It was satisfying to see it develop into a colorful piece of art. Later, we all went to her birthday celebration and, along with the crowds, paraded past the front steps of the palace, where the royal family stood. We stopped in front of them while a couple of children from our group presented the Queen with the handiwork. We were all very proud.

When I was nine and the time neared for another trip to the country, I became almost ill with anxiety. My parents urged the authorities to make alternate arrangements for me. For the sake of my mental well-being, they sent me to a small town to stay with a family that had six children. This turned out to be one of the best summers of my young life.

I received an abundance of love and good food. The spaciousness of the town was in sharp contrast to the cramped quarters of the city streets. There was a calmness, a quietude—no echoes of shouting children and quarreling neighbors reverberating off the walls of narrow streets. Here there was the green of grass and trees. Here I could breathe more freely.

I became good friends with the children. We played for endless hours in the sunshine. I learned how to ride a bike, something I had always dreamed of doing. Every couple of days, a group of us walked to the fields outside the town to gather clover for the pet rabbits. On Sundays we worshiped in a cathedral, sitting in the pew that had my host family's name engraved on the plaque. The church was huge, and I felt very small under its high ceiling. Our stately hymns were swallowed up by the cavernous interior. During the sermon, the mom gave us peppermints to suck on.

The six weeks went by far too quickly. I was almost sorry when it came time to go home.

I was born in the same two-room flat my family lived in until my ninth year. It was on the second floor of a row house in a rundown, noisy neighborhood of Amsterdam. A big table stood in the center of the living room, covered by the traditional Dutch carpet-thick tablecloth. The room doubled as my parents' bedroom. During the day, their bed leaned against the wall, hidden behind a curtain. The second room held two beds: a double one for my younger sister, Ineke, and me and a single one for my half-sister, Ann. We had a few toys and a small collection of books. Our favorites were a series of Dutch comic books which our Uncle Meindert, the bookbinder, had bound into thick, hard-covered volumes for us.

Our kitchen was a narrow space where Mom cooked on a two-burner hotplate. No oven, no refrigerator and no hot running water. The toilet, or WC (water closet), was in a tiny space off the kitchen. Having no shower or bathtub, my mother heated water on the hotplate for our baths each Saturday night, pouring it into a galvanized tub which she had placed on the living room floor. After our bath, we shivered in our pajamas as we ate our standard Saturday night dinner of rice with butter and brown sugar.

The main part of our diet was bread. We had sliced bread for breakfast and sliced bread for lunch. Like most other Dutch folk, we spread it with almost anything. We used cheese or cold cuts when we could afford them, but the favorite spreads—especially for us children—were sweet: jam, peanut butter and chocolate paste. Other favorites were chocolate and colored sugar sprinkles, such as those used in North America for cake decorations. If none of these was available, we'd substitute brown or white sugar, sliced bananas or apples, or the wafer-thin spicy speculaas cookies.

Sunday was the only day we ate meat, most often one large meatball for each of us. The rest of the week, our dinners might consist of mashed mixtures of potatoes and sauerkraut, potatoes and apple sauce or potatoes with grated onions and carrots. Oddly enough, in spite of the limited supply of nutritional food, our household saw no shortage of cookies, chocolate and candy. This suggests to me that the reason for the undernourishment our family suffered was not simply lack of money—though that was partly to blame—but ignorance of the importance of a healthy diet. Our family's eating habits were common in postwar Holland. It was an era when the many sources of health information we have available to us today in magazines and on television did not exist. My parents' poor education did not help matters. Both my mother and father went only as far as grade six.

I'm sure it was the deficiency in our diet that was responsible for the poor health I suffered when I was young. I spent long stretches in bed with a variety of illnesses. At one time, canker sores covered the top and bottom of my tongue and the roof of my mouth, likely the result of malnutrition. The pain was excruciating. I was admitted to hospital where nurses spent long periods trying to feed me lukewarm soup, one painful spoonful after another.

Throughout my first ten years, I spent much time in hospitals, experiences that disturbed me deeply. I was fearful of unfamiliar situations and afraid to be away from home. Visiting opportunities, even for the youngest patients, were limited to one brief hour or so per day. I remember lonely, tearful periods in hospital beds. My mother was also frequently ill and unable to care for us. My sister and I often had to stay with friends and relatives.

When we emigrated to Canada, conditions improved significantly, though my young life was never easy.

## Where Did My Mood Disorder Come From?

A FEW YEARS ago, when I was reviewing collections of family photographs, I came across two that were identical, except that in one of them the image of my father's sister had been cut away with scissors. This aunt had spent most of her adult life in a mental hospital and died there. I know that the family was ashamed of this. She was seldom mentioned. The discovery was a revelation to me and a clear indication of the extent of the disgrace such illness brought—even within my father's family, one I had always considered a loving one.

In spite of having what is probably the same disease as my aunt had, I was not overly distressed by the cut-up photograph. Fortunately, I have come to understand my disorder well. I know it is not a reflection of my worth as a person. This helped me not take the photograph personally. Nevertheless, I was shocked by this glaring evidence of the rejection individuals can experience as a result of stigma.

According to the National Institute of Mental Health, more than two-thirds of people who have bipolar disorder have at least one close family member with it or with unipolar depression. The disorder often skips a generation and does not affect everyone in the family. Not everyone with the condition has relatives with mood disorders.

Many studies are underway to determine which genes are responsible for the disorder. When the answer is found, diagnosis will be simpler and easier; treatment will be more easily tailored to the individual; and early intervention and prevention will reduce the severity of the illness.

In my case, it's clear that my father's family carried the genes that caused me to have the disorder. Evidence in some of his brothers' and sisters' lives suggests it. I have an aunt, a cousin and a sister, all diagnosed with bipolar disorder. Depression has affected a number of other family members.

As many are aware, creativity is a frequent by-product of manic depression, a fact I find fascinating and can clearly see in my own life. (I will explore this phenomenon in Chapter 9.) This, of course, does not necessarily mean that all creative individuals have mental illness. Yet the abundance of giftedness my father's family displayed in music, fine art, dance, architecture and story-telling makes me wonder whether there was not more illness present than I knew of. People did, especially in the first half of the twentieth century, tend to keep such things quiet. I also believe there must be individuals who have mild bipolar symptoms, but who would not be classified as having an illness because they are able to function normally. Perhaps some have the strong moods but are never diagnosed.

My aunts, uncles and cousins were lively, passionate people. I have fond memories of Sunday afternoons, crowded into Uncle Chris and Aunt Sara's flat. With the aroma of freshly ground coffee in the air, we visited. We often sang as my uncle played his organ. We enjoyed well-told stories, magic stunts from an older cousin and tricks from the dog, Blackie. And the laughter! There weren't enough chairs for the children, but we found many a welcoming lap to crawl into.

I've always taken pride in our family's talents and skills. One uncle built an ornately carved dining room table, chairs and china cabinet. Another had a little doll factory in his backyard shed. On one of my visits back to Amsterdam, an architect cousin showed us the plans for his latest restoration work on a cathedral. A vivacious cousin was a story-teller extraordinaire who was often asked to perform at weddings. His sons would be part of the entertainment, playing their music as the guests sang and danced their way around the room in long meandering rows.

My younger sister, Ineke, who also has bipolar disorder, is musical, in the past having composed her own music on the piano. She had no trouble playing this instrument in spite of never having had a lesson. Ineke spent a short time as a professional dancer and opened her own dance studio. As she got older and no longer able to dance, she did some sculpting, creating bold depictions of the human form in concrete.

And then there was my father. Moving to Canada meant that, for the first time in his life, he had plenty of space to set up an easel. He usually had a painting on the go and was at his happiest when he had the opportunity to work on his art.

## Our Family's Faith

ALTHOUGH I WAS raised in a Christian home, we were not a family that went to church together. During my first ten years, the years after the Second World War, my parents spent Sunday mornings with a group of friends, singing gospel songs and preaching from the Bible on Amsterdam street corners. Meanwhile, my half-sister, Annie, who is ten years older than me, took Ineke and me to Sunday school at a Pentecostal church.

My parents were devoted to their group of evangelical friends, spending much time with them. Dad regularly hoisted the big wooden box containing his organ on his shoulder and traveled the trams with Mom to song practices and to hospital and prison visits.

I remember the choir practices in our cramped flat. One time when I was a toddler, I wanted to sing along. I frantically tried to find the song in the hymnal, but of course—not yet able to read—couldn't. I cried bitterly, feeling left out.

Dad copied music, drawing the staff by hand on stencils and then copying out the notes for the songs the group planned to sing. We had their portable mimeograph machine at home with which he made copies. He also used that machine for the occasional newsletter. I well remember the mess of inky newspapers that protected our living room table and the ugly night-blue stains covering his long fingers. He had no concern in those days about copyright laws. In fact, I'm sure that no one we knew had ever heard of such a thing.

At Christmas time, this group assembled fruit baskets and small handmade gifts to bring to underprivileged families. When I think of it now, I'm amazed at how my parents could have managed that, since we ourselves were poor and lacking adequate food and clothing. It occurred to me, though, when I was reading 2 Corinthians 8:2–3, that their situation was much like that of the Macedonian Christians whom Paul spoke of when he wrote, *"Out of the most severe trial, their overflowing joy and their extreme poverty welled up in rich generosity...they gave as much as they were able, and even beyond their ability."*

My parents had also experienced severe trials. Only a couple of years earlier, they had survived the Nazi occupation. They had suffered to the point of starvation. Near the end of the war, soldiers had taken Dad to Germany to work, but he escaped. I can imagine the joy they must have felt when the country was liberated. I can imagine how they must have thanked God and how they would have wanted to express this gratitude by sharing God's love with others.

When we came to Canada, we went to a Dutch Reformed church for a short while, my father becoming the choir leader. But my parents did not feel at home there and left a couple of years later. They missed the evangelical work they had so loved to do in their homeland. A family friend began taking Ineke and me to a Baptist Church for Sunday school while Mom and Dad stayed home. Many years later, when their language skills had improved, they finally began to attend and feel comfortable in a non-denominational, English-speaking congregation in Vancouver.

During my youth at Sunday school, I had never felt moved to accept Jesus as my Savior, though the opportunity was often presented. I sometimes wonder why but believe I was just not ready to make that decision with genuine understanding. As I became a teen, it became even more difficult to believe the church's teachings, though I did not stop going to church. One day someone persuaded me to teach Sunday school. Feeling pressured, I took on the job in spite of not being a believer.

I have always loved children, and I learned to tell Bible stories in an animated way, becoming quite good at holding the attention of the dozen preschoolers in my class. But it was not in me to be dishonest and to teach things I could not believe myself. I told the stories but skipped the parts that spoke of the power and love of God. I omitted explaining the lessons that the stories were intended to teach. For two years, I hung on, knowing that what I was doing wasn't right. But, being a timid girl, I couldn't find the courage to leave. Finally, as I entered grade thirteen, I resigned, with the convenient excuse that school was going to keep me too busy.

I left the church and did not go back until I was in my early forties.

## We Emigrate to Canada

IN 1956, WHEN I was ten years old, we packed our most valued belongings into a huge wooden crate, and our family boarded the Waterman, a converted freighter bound for Halifax. We followed countless other Dutch families drawn to Canada by the promise of a better life. Many, our family included, had never recovered economically from the Second World War. Ever since Canada's forces liberated Holland from Nazi occupation, a mere ten years earlier, our people loved Canadians and trusted their country to be an amiable one.

The Alexander family, good friends of ours, had made the move a couple of years earlier and sent glowing reports of the richness of this country. In Vancouver, where they had settled, there was no one without the luxuries of a refrigerator, hot running water and a bathtub. And many owned a television set, an item almost unheard of in Amsterdam homes.

We survived a rough nine-day crossing of the Atlantic, the small ship rocking constantly on the waves. Almost everyone suffered from seasickness. Those who weren't sick, including Dad, nursed the ones who were. They brought us to the deck to spend hours lying in chairs in the fresh air. We tried hard to somehow make our stomachs behave. Instead of the good meals we knew awaited us in the dining room, we were only able to eat dry biscuits, a paper bag always at the ready. Dad kept busy running from one end of the ship to the other, cheering passengers with his comical ways as he helped out in whatever way he could. He brought blankets and made sure everyone had a package of biscuits. I was proud of my dad.

Deep in the hold of the ship, next to the engine room with its constant clamor, were the women and children's quarters. The dorm was crowded with bunk beds, spaced four feet apart. Eight-year-old Ineke was excited to get a top bunk. But during a particularly rough night, the rocking rolled her back and forth so much that she fell out, suffering a minor concussion. In the bottom bunk, poor Mom spent most of the voyage in bed trying to deal with migraine headaches as well as seasickness.

I treasure the memory of an occasion when, on calmer waters, Dad and I spent some quiet time on deck in the dark of night. In the middle of the ocean, miles from nearest land, we admired the awesome canopy of stars above us. I felt very small.

After a ten day voyage, we arrived in Halifax and boarded a train for the last leg of our journey. This was an immigrants' train. We didn't have the luxuries of sleeping berths or dining cars. Instead, we tried our best to sleep on the hard wooden benches. Once in a while the train stopped at a station that had a small store attached. Dad would run in and hastily buy us a few sandwiches and snacks. In a corner of the railcar, a baby cried constantly as it swung in a small hammock suspended from the ceiling.

Traveling through the Rockies was the highlight of the trip, especially for Dad. He marveled at the beauty of the towering mountains. The quantity of water in the rushing rivers and the cascading waterfalls amazed him. I can still remember the awe in his voice as he expressed his feelings about all that he saw. He had such a sensitive spirit that I'm sure he could have been a writer if he had been more fortunate and received a better education.

I often think of this appreciation for nature my father taught me at times such as these. From him I learned to respect and never take for granted the beauties of God's creation. Ineke, only eight at the time of our trip, does not remember much of it. But, thanks to the awareness Dad instilled in us, she does clearly recall how she admired the Rocky Mountains. A year later, still struggling with the English language, she stood in front of her class and brought tears to her teacher's eyes as she described the mountains as she remembered them.

After three days and four nights on the train, we finally arrived at our new home. The entire Alexander family stood on the station platform to welcome us. Were we ever happy to see them!

# New Canadians

THE ADJUSTMENTS WE had to make to this new country were huge, though more so for my parents than for us children. As our sponsors, our friends were supportive. They helped us find a place to live and learn our way around, and they showed us how to use the bus transportation. On Sunday nights, we visited them at their home to watch the Ed Sullivan Show on television and eat Canadian snacks.

Dad needed to find a job immediately. With not enough money to spare for bus fare, he walked five miles to downtown Vancouver each morning in search of something he could do. I can imagine how difficult this must have been for him as a forty-four-year-old man. He spoke no English and knew nothing about the city's business scene. Eventually he did get his first job, working at the Regis Hotel doing maintenance work.

Things were difficult for Mom as well. Learning how to shop for and cook the new foods was not easy for someone forty-two years old. She missed her friends and family. Because it took a long time for our crate of belongings to arrive, she was forced to buy things we couldn't really afford. We immediately went into debt buying furnishings for the apartment. Although Mom did go to an English language class with Dad, she found it too much of a struggle and did not persevere. For a while, Mom suffered from a severe case of culture shock.

For Ineke and me, it was not quite so difficult. Although we knew no English, we quickly picked it up. I went to a New Canadian class, part of an elementary school program. Seven-year-old Ineke, considered too young for this, was placed in a kindergarten class. Being a bright little girl, she moved to her appropriate grade level within months.

When I first arrived, I couldn't believe that we were indeed in the city of Vancouver. It looked to me as though we were out in the country. Amsterdam did not have such greenery except in some of the parks: no lawns, gardens and trees. The streets of my new home city were wide, and the houses were low, with spaces separating them and front yards and back yards. What richness!

We were introduced to toast, potato chips and apple pie. Getting used to Orange Crush and Coca Cola took a while. The fizzy bubbles hurt our tongue. When Mom and Dad were invited for an evening visit by some new acquaintances, they were perplexed when, instead of being offered coffee as soon as they arrived, as they would be in a Dutch home, they had to wait until nine o'clock to receive refreshments.

Our sister, Ann, at the age of twenty, also had a rough time in her new country. One year after our arrival, she married our friends' son, Albert Alexander. Learning to cook Canadian foods took a while for her. Not having an oven during her initial years of marriage didn't help. The first time she cooked a turkey—a food item that had been unknown to us in Holland—she cut it into pieces as one would cut up a chicken. Then she proceeded to fry them in a pan. She worked at it for a long time, but the meat would not cook through. Eventually she had to throw the entire bird into the garbage can.

When we rented our first house, we did not realize that lawns had to be taken care of. Only when a neighbor suggested that perhaps it was time to cut the lawn did Mom give Ineke and me some shears with which to cut the eight-inch high grass covering our over-sized lot. We didn't get very far. When the apple trees supplied us with their harvest, Mom sent us into the neighborhood to sell the fruit door to door.

In order to afford renting a house and to make it possible for my mother to have some work she was capable of doing, we took in boarders. These were usually single Dutch men. Thus, for most of my growing up years in Canada, our family did not have a private life. We shared our living room and kitchen table with others. In the evening, Ineke and I had tall stacks of dishes to wash, and, on the weekends, we often made three beds besides our own. I didn't complain about this lifestyle, though, looking back on it now, I wonder what a normal family life would have been like.

# My Teen Years

MY TEENS WERE not a happy time. More often than not, I felt unbearably forlorn. I was shy, had few friends and was afraid to speak out in class. I did not fit in with the liveliness happening around me. The only way I could bear going to school was by creating a game, promising myself—trying to believe—that after each bad day there would be a good day. Good day...bad day...good day...bad day...and so on. That is how I survived.

I didn't go to parties or participate in sports or other extracurricular activities. My favorite out-of-school pastimes were to read and to maintain a stamp collection. Although I became an extremely creative person in adulthood, I had no interest in art at this time. I looked out at the world, observing but not participating.

Today I can recognize that I was suffering from depression. Yet in those days, there was little talk about this common mental disorder. There was little understanding about such things.

Living in a sheltered home environment with parents who did not understand the ways of their new country did not help my situation. While I was between the ages of ten and twenty, our family moved seven times. I didn't have a chance to put down roots and only made a couple of lasting friendships.

Yet, while I was not able to break through my subdued outer shell, within me vibrant ambition waited to be tapped. Though school was not a pleasant place for me socially, by the end of summer holidays my love of learning always made me look forward to going back. I enjoyed the challenge. My dream was to be a grade one or two teacher, a dream that had been with me since early childhood.

I aimed for A's in school and often earned them, though my overall average was only a B. I believe that if my attendance had been more regular, I might have achieved the A average I tried for. I frequently missed school due to illness, not—I can see now—always stemming from physical sources. From the time I began to have periods, anemia became a constant problem. This contributed significantly to my health problems. At the age of 38, I had a hysterectomy, and my blood count finally went up to the normal level of 120. Only then did I discover that much of my tiredness, something I had attributed to depression, had been due to anemia.

Because my mother wasn't able to write in English, I always had to write her notes to the teacher explaining why I hadn't been at school. Then I had her sign them. This was not easy for me. I didn't always know what to say. I found it hard to come up with something original each time. How nice it would have been to have had a mother who could have done this for me!

Ineke likes to call me a controller, and I guess I do have that tendency and had it even back then. When I was sixteen, I enjoyed organizing a Christmas party for our family and friends, the way I envisioned a Christmas should be celebrated. I loved to organize in the safety of my own home. Ineke wasn't sure she wanted to be a part of all this, but I was able to talk her into helping me with the preparations. Although I had almost no experience as a cook, we spent many hours baking in the kitchen. We decorated the living room and found copies of the words to the most popular Christmas carols. At the party, Ineke and I did all the serving and made sure that everyone joined in the carol singing.

A friend and I warded off summer boredom by organizing a small play group for neighborhood children. Several times we led them in songs and craft activities. Both of us loved children, and it was a good way to pass the long days of summer while providing free time for their parents.

In spite of the placid girl I presented to the world, the "real me" was often dramatic, making appearances within the privacy of my bedroom. Powerful music such as Gershwin's *Rhapsody in Blue* was my favorite. I played my recording of it over and over. I also found great joy in conducting the Vienna State Opera Orchestra in their performance of Strauss's *Fledermaus Overture*. After I saw Mary Martin on stage in *Sound of Music, Climb Every Mountain* became a song that I sang often. I truly believed that I could climb mountains, follow rainbows and would find my dreams.

Instead of entering university immediately after high school graduation, I decided to do grade thirteen, the equivalent of the first year of university. This was a more affordable way to begin my post-secondary education. A couple of good friends were doing the same. Here, for the first time in my life, I finally broke out of my shell. I made many friends, enjoyed my classes and had fun.

At the end of the days' classes, instead of going home, a bunch of us stayed in the library every night until it closed at nine o'clock. I was better able to study in this environment than at home. Being the only member of the family to go past grade nine, I was a mystery to my parents as a student. Their lives had been so different from mine. When I did go home, I was expected to take part in the household chores, looking after the boarders' needs. For someone like me, someone who had to struggle to get good grades, trying to study at home would have been difficult.

The social aspects of spending the entire day at school were probably even more important to me than the studying. For the first time in my life, I felt like I fit in. I enjoyed the freedom not possible at home. Each night four to six of us had dinner in the school cafeteria. I could afford no more than French fries, but they filled me up.

During that grade thirteen year, I also had my first boyfriend, a big adjustment for a girl who had always been afraid of boys. I was thrilled to actually have a young man interested in me. With the shell I had built around me, the romantic relationships that other girls enjoyed had been out of reach for me. This man was not the ideal kind of friend to have, and I think I might have been better off without him. But we spent a good part of the summer together, and I enjoyed going to the beach in his car and doing the kinds of things everyone my age was doing.

At the end of a free and easy summer, I started university. Here is where my bipolar disorder first became evident in a dramatic way. I became psychotic and lost touch with reality. It was bound to become a factor in my life, but I believe the stress and change I was going through triggered it at this time. I wonder if that is why so many of us first become sick at the age of nineteen or twenty, the period of transition between youth and adulthood.

# I Lose Touch

TODAY MY DIAGNOSIS is Bipolar Type 1 disorder. Psychosis, similar to the psychosis suffered by individuals with schizophrenia, is part of it. Antipsychotic medication will control these symptoms, but not being on such medication at the time, I broke completely from reality.

I clearly recall the tortured feelings of physical and mental agitation—sitting scrunched up on the living room sofa, hugging my knees to my body, trying everything I could to still my restlessness, searching for peace. I struggled to concentrate on the Shirley Temple movies playing on our black and white television, hoping they would take my mind off my discomfort. In my delusional state, I felt I had to watch them because I believed the series of old films was being aired especially for me. At times I resorted to hitting my head against the wall as hard as I could in an effort to end the torment.

One day at a church fall fair, as I watched the people at the booths, each face I looked at appeared twisted, ugly and evil. I searched for a friendly expression but couldn't find one.

My mind was trapped so that everything I perceived was distorted and without reason. I could not connect with reality. My mother and father held me between them in their bed, taking turns to pray for me. Nothing helped.

Evenings were the worst times. Rustling noises outside frightened me, though, even now, I don't know if they were actually there or in my imagination. I believed they were caused by men crawling around outside the house, men trying to find a way to get at me. In a panic, and in defiance of my parents who tried to stop me, I called my family doctor at his home, begging for help. "I'm scared. There are people after me. What can I do?" Strangely, although what I went through seemed real to me, I knew I was going mad and that what I experienced was not actually the way things were. Nevertheless, the fear and agony continued to grip my entire being. I couldn't stop it.

My doctor was angry that I called. "Marja, in my office yesterday, you indicated that you understood what was happening in your head. That means you are going to be okay. You just won't believe it." In his mind, recognizing my problem meant that I should also be able to control it. But, much as I wanted to, I couldn't.

I had nowhere to turn. My doctor did not believe in psychiatrists, expressing his opinion that they were quacks. He thought I should be able to overcome this on my own. This is how some people felt towards psychiatry in the sixties, when this "mysterious" field of medicine was not as well understood as it is today. Some doctors were even suspicious of it.

Without treatment, my psychosis escalated until I had to be admitted, in great distress, to the emergency department of our local hospital. Here I was given a shot to put me to sleep. When I awoke hours later, I found myself in a hospital ward lined by two rows of six or eight beds each, the covers neatly smoothed. Picking up the chart that lay on the bedside table next to me, I read the header: CREASE CLINIC.

# Hospital Days[*]

THE NINE MONTHS I spent in that hospital were traumatic. Thank God, the conditions I experienced forty years ago seldom exists

---

[*] In 2005 I obtained my medical records from the provincial archives to ensure that I could write a factual account about this fuzzy past.

any longer in the western world. Psychiatric medicine has come a long way since then.

Crease Clinic was a monstrous brick building with barred windows. It formed part of what was called Essondale, a name feared by patients and the object of insensitive jokes by others. Today, six large buildings sit on the park-like site and are collectively called Riverview Hospital. My memories of those dreadful months are vague.

I do recall countless snatches of events: cleaning the toilets and mopping the floors; lining up for medications when the bell rang; the woman who insisted on smoking in bed, setting her mattress on fire three nights in a row. (I was so heavily medicated that I slept through each fire.) I remember the rows of beds, out of bounds except for sleeping. I remember my yearning for privacy.

Most of all I recall the way I felt. I could not communicate much. I was like a huge blob. I believe now that this might have been due to over-medication rather than depression. The more dysfunctional I was, the more pills I received. The more pills I received, the more dysfunctional I became. Finally the doctor reduced my medication and prescribed a series of shock treatments. These made me well enough to leave the hospital.

Acute psychosis that had descended upon me had gradually brought me to this institution. During my entire time there, my diagnosis was schizophrenia. (Much later in life, my doctor changed this diagnosis to Bipolar Type 1.) I was frightened and disconnected from reality.

My records laid part of the blame on family conditions and overprotective parenting. This rationalization for mental illness was the norm in the sixties. I am now sure I would have become sick eventually, no matter how well my mother and father raised me. Today the medical community understands this disorder as a biological condition which can and does affect all levels of society: "good" families, the rich, the famous, the educated and uneducated.

During my first few days at the institution, I ate my meals at a table by a window overlooking the highway and train tracks. I was convinced that men were hiding in the bushes on the other side of the tracks. I felt their rifles trained on me, ready to shoot at any time. In an effort to hide from them, I pulled down the blinds. Only then could I feel safe. But other patients repeatedly opened them, and I would once more feel dangerously exposed. I constantly expected to hear shots to ring out.

Marching up and down the hall, safely away from those windows, I courageously sang "Onward, Christian soldiers, marching as to war, with the cross of Jesus going on before…Forward into battle, see His banners go!" I made myself as tall as I could and faced straight ahead, determined to show my enemies that I was not afraid. How I wished I could remember the rest of those words! Another patient occasionally joined me. We held hands as we walked together, up and down the dim hallway.

My relentless state of anxiety exhausted me. I tried my hardest to rest but couldn't. Sitting still was impossible. In the lounge, I sat on my hands, trying to keep my body from incessant squirming, but nothing worked. How I wished I could rest—to have some comfort and security.

It was November, and the Greater Vancouver area had received an early snowfall. This was an unusual event here, a part of the country often referred to as Canada's California. I had improved enough to accompany a nurse and a handful of other patients for a walk in the crisp fresh air. A brilliant white splendor covered the rolling lawns and hung in the trees. I was overwhelmed by the dream-like world surrounding me. The misery that had enveloped me turned to wonder. I gasped, scarcely able to catch my breath. Seagulls cried out as they landed a short distance ahead of us, flurries of dirty white playing on the clean snow.

This brief venture into the outdoors was difficult to cope with. But it was a beginning. Eight days after admission, I was allowed to sign out for short walks on the grounds by myself.

Three months later, my condition improved to a level where my doctor considered me well enough to try living in the community again. I went back to the office where I had worked, openly telling the manager what had happened to me. He let me work a few hours a day to begin with. Gradually I was able to increase to full time.

I had good care during my first hospital stay. Dr. Gerald McDougall was in charge of my case. He was a compassionate person who always had time to talk when I felt I needed to tell him things. Soon afterward he went into private practice, and I began seeing him in his Vancouver office.

However, when I tried going back to university seven months after my release, the stress caused my psychotic symptoms to reappear. I returned to Crease Clinic, this time without Dr. McDougall. My new doctor did not even interview me. When I passed him in the hall and smiled at him, he didn't smile back. My records contain only one brief report by him, which he wrote at the time of my final discharge six months later.

One big surprise, a painful one my records revealed, was a letter from a partner in Dr. McDougall's private practice. After an interview with me a couple of days following my second admission, he wrote, "There would seem little point in this girl remaining in hospital...and since her previous employer...seems to have an interest in her, and is prepared to tolerate her limited functioning, it may be best that she at least be given a trial with them. When she is in a more normal environment she may yet progress a little further..."

Only recently, when I studied these records, did I become aware of this letter. Apparently no one read it, paid attention to it or believed it to be the correct course of action. I remained in hospital for another six months. I was dismayed to learn that those long months of over-medication and eventual shock treatments might have been avoided.

The doctor's report revealed something else I had not known about. Bert Cowan, the manager of the office where I had worked, was willing to give me an opportunity to try working again in spite of my poor condition. I had not known the full extent of this man's generous spirit. His kindness after my final discharge from hospital would later help me rehabilitate.

Remembering those months is not pleasant. Reviewing my records from that period disturbed and angered me. But when I'd had time to think about it, I could see that what I went through helped make me the person I am today. I have learned what it is to be down and out. I have learned what it is to lose self-esteem. My illness and my hospital experiences taught me compassion for others. Reading my records reminded me how serious my condition had been and how far I've come. Knowing what my records showed about me, I am more grateful than ever for the full and vibrant life I now have. God has been good to me.

# Wes

I MET WES at a party during the seven months between my two stays at Crease Clinic. We began spending time with each other. We went for drives in his Triumph sports car and had long talks, though I believe I did most of the talking. By the time I became sick again and had to be re-admitted to hospital, we had become good friends. And Wes stuck with me.

When I became well enough to be allowed weekend passes, we spent much of that time together. Wes loved to drive. He loved getting away from the city to explore areas around Vancouver. Enjoying the outside world—the real world—felt good. It felt good to be with someone who cared enough to be with me.

At that time, I looked and acted like someone who was mentally ill. I was over-medicated and it showed. My mouth hung open a lot of the time. Yet Wes did not show any shame. He took me to a party, a coffeehouse and occasional movies. Looking back,

I know it must have taken courage for him to do all this. Few young men would have done likewise.

Sunday nights he returned me to the hospital, walking me into the great brick building, up the stairs and down the hall to the heavy locked door of my ward. We were always a bit late and had to bang hard on the door for someone to let me in. After a hug, I returned to my existence inside, and Wes returned to his life on the outside.

Wes has never made it a secret that he had other dates during the time I was in hospital. This was good, healthy and normal for him, and I'm glad he did. In fact, this early stage of our relationship was not a terribly romantic one. Our friendship did not turn into love for quite a while. I first needed to become emotionally well and rid of the excessive medication that kept me from being a truly alive person.

After my discharge from hospital, our friendship continued. Our love grew slowly and steadily into what is even today, a beautiful thing. Neither of us proposed marriage. It was a given that we would marry. We were totally devoted to each other and knew that we would spend the rest of our lives together. In May of 1969, two years after I left the hospital, we were married.

God was good to bring me this patient, even-tempered and faithful man. If Wes ever lost hope that I would become a fully functioning person, a wife with whom he could share a happy home, he didn't show it. Having been with me almost from the beginning of my troubles, he understands my disorder fully, sometimes better than my doctors do. He is able to warn me when he sees me taking on too many responsibilities. He endures my depressions, never openly giving up on me. When I'm not able to function well enough to look after my normal household work, he doesn't complain. He realizes that I always do the best I can.

But when I get sick, he suffers as well. At such times, his mood can hover dangerously close to depression. When I see this happening, I feel a sense of responsibility and work even harder to recover. We work together on the grocery shopping, cooking and washing up, jobs I would normally do on my own. By pooling our resources, we build each other up, gathering energy from each other. Not only do we complete the essential household chores, our social interaction helps the healing process.

Wes has always had good jobs to support us and to help us enjoy a comfortable life. Once our son was born, I didn't have to participate in earning the family income. This left me free to use my time for the things I most loved to do: my cooking, photography and many other hobbies. I had lots of time and energy to be the kind of mother I wanted to be for Jeff.

What a blessing to have had this opportunity to live without excessive pressure and to be free to organize my days in whatever ways I wished! The lack of structure was at times difficult to deal with, though. Sometimes I felt downright bored and would have welcomed a job. I tried part-time work a few times, but the stress was too much, and I did not keep it up for long.

Wes and I are very much individuals. We share some activities, and others we count our own. Although I am a Christian and go to church, Wes has not followed this path. Photography and membership in a camera club have been important in both of our lives since we got married. We've enjoyed many camping holidays together, as well as trips abroad.

But Wes has a great deal more desire for adventure than I have. Unlike me, he'd like to see as much of the world as he possibly can. As a result, he frequently takes trips without me. He'd love to take me along, but often the stress of travel prevents me from going. Sometimes I can't cope with the excitement of traveling to foreign countries such Bali and Guatemala. Yet I would never want to keep Wes from what is important to him. So, oftentimes, while Wes finds adventure in the big wide world, I stay comfortably at home, spending time with friends and receiving stimulation from my creative projects.

Wes and I, like most couples, have times when our relationship needs work. We've had our struggles but have been able to resolve them. He has been and continues to be indispensable to me as husband, friend and supporter. I love him dearly, never forgetting how he stood by me through thick and thin. Yet although I have at times had to lean heavily on him, I'm happy that I've also learned to become a free and independent individual.

## Becoming a Mother

ON ST. NICHOLAS EVE, at the age of five years, I received my doll, a rubber one with brown eyes. St. Nicholas had placed it, along with all the other gifts for our family, in a white cotton sack outside the door to our flat. Marijka was the first doll of significance for me, and I still remember how ecstatic I was when I opened the shoebox in which she was wrapped. I don't think I desired any other doll after receiving this one. There was no need for another one. I had to work hard enough just to take care of her: dressing her each morning, feeding her and putting her to bed at night. I loved being a mother.

A couple of times, I did something I had been warned not to: I gave Marijka milk to drink through the opening in her mouth. I had thought that would be alright. She had a pee-hole at the bottom, and the milk would be able to come out again. But she did not smell good after that, and Dad had to take my poor doll apart and wash the insides. Her head, arms, legs and body lay in pieces for a long time until the insides were good and dry. For days and days, I would beg Dad to put her together again. It was tough seeing Marijka in such a condition.

I faithfully played with this doll until I was ten years old. She came with me on the boat from Holland, the only toy that wasn't packed into the shipping crate. In recent years, she has sat on a dresser in our bedroom, still wearing some of the clothes Mom had made for her. And currently, she is safely tucked away in a box in the basement, along with other treasures I can't part with.

When Wes and I had been married for three years, I begged him to allow me to fulfill the role of motherhood I had always envisioned for myself. I very much wanted a baby. I didn't believe my life could be complete without a child to raise. He hesitated for a long time. Today, when I look back at the mental difficulties that were so much a part of my life, I can understand why. But eventually he gave in, and I stopped taking the pill, becoming pregnant soon after.

How I grinned on the bus ride home from the doctor's office after I had been told I was going to have a baby! I could not maintain my composure. People must have wondered about me that day!

But with the pregnancy came severe health problems. I had to stop taking my medications, the medications I needed to function normally. Neither was I eating as healthily as a pregnant woman should. By the time I was four months along, I had spiraled downward and was admitted to the Vancouver General Hospital psychiatric ward. Not only was I psychotic, the anemia that had plagued me since my teens had severely weakened me. My psychiatrist ordered lots of rest—no running around as I'd been doing.

At the hospital, a nutritionist spent some time with me, outlining the foods I should be sure to eat. My antipsychotic medication was started again, in spite of the possible detriment to the baby. It was impossible for me to continue living without the treatment I needed. What good would I be as a mother if I ended up in an institution?

I worked hard to recover during those couple of weeks at the hospital. All my thoughts, plans and activities were focused on the role I knew lay ahead of me. I worked on cross-stitch projects as therapy for my active mind. I suffered through the adjustment of eating All-Bran cereal every morning. (It tasted like cardboard, but even now I continue having it at breakfast.) Once I became well enough, I went for walks around the hospital grounds in an effort to become physically stronger, a little further each day. When Wes made his daily visits, I did all I could to help him have faith in me as a good wife for him and a good mother for our child. I even baked peanut butter cookies for him in the ward's little kitchen. What he must have gone through during those weeks!

After Jeff's birth, I went through yet another period of psychosis. He left hospital before I did, spending the first while with his Grandma Bergen. When I was finally discharged from hospital and we picked him up from her, I was nervous. Still not completely rehabilitated, I now had to adjust to my new role as mother as well. "I'm not sure I'll know what to do," I confided in Mom Bergen before getting into the car with the baby in my arms. "Just love him," she said, visibly fighting off tears as she turned to go back into the house. I never forgot that advice.

For the weeks following, Dr. McDougall asked me to visit him twice a week, along with the baby. I thought that kind of attention from him was rather excessive, but I can now see that he wanted to make sure I was able to care for the baby as I should. He also asked a public health nurse to look in on me regularly. This nurse encouraged me to volunteer at the local baby clinic that operated at a school close by. I welcomed those outings.

## Our Baby Grows

FORTUNATELY, JEFF WAS a good baby, grew to be an easy boy to care for and a teen who caused little trouble. Today he is an adult I am proud of. He has high moral standards and a giving nature.

To be perfectly truthful, I didn't find the first eighteen months with our new baby as exciting as most mothers do. Perhaps I was depressed, preventing me from appreciating that time as well as I could have. But I looked forward to a child I could talk to, read stories to and teach. I had loved young children all my life, in later years even becoming an accomplished child photographer, but I did not relate to babies as well as I did to older children. I couldn't wait for him to grow into someone I could do more interesting things with.

When he was five months old, I packed him in the carrier on my back and traveled the bus downtown to buy him his first book. With that purchase, we started a bedtime reading ritual that we seldom missed and continued until he was about seven years old. He learned to love books.

When he decided he wanted to explore the kitchen cupboards, I allowed him one cupboard for himself, the one that held the pots. He had lots of fun banging on those pots with a wooden spoon. And so, before his first birthday, his love of drumming was born. This was to lead to his playing a full set of drums in his teens.

At eighteen months or so, one of our favorite activities was to draw together. With Jeff on my lap, I sat at the kitchen table while I drew pictures, telling stories about them as I did so. He learned how to use a pencil and get it to do what he wanted before the age of two. Now I was really enjoying myself. I loved to teach.

As a toddler, Jeff accompanied us on photography expeditions with his own camera in hand, a broken-down box camera. He took pictures like we did but without the film. Eventually it became only fair to give him a point-and-shoot camera with real film in it. He wasn't bad at all. When we took him out of school at the age of eight to go to Greece with us, we made him work. We assigned him the job of taking a series of slides of our travels and preparing a travelog for his grade two class. Later he showed a good set of pictures, complete with informative details he had researched.

Through every season of Jeff's life, I encouraged creativity. He did not get many coloring books from us, but we gave him ample paper, pencils, paint, modeling clay, Lego and, of course, film. When we took him along to a photography meeting or gallery, a new pad of paper and fresh pencils kept him happily occupied.

My efforts to make him into a creative person have paid off. I'm happy about that. Today he is a computer programmer with an interest in music, architecture and film-making. He loves books, has a big collection of his own and enjoys his part-time work at the Vancouver Public Library, surrounded by them. He married Jeannette, a graphic designer. Together they operate a web design business.

One thing I regret is that I was never able to help him get ready for school. Throughout his elementary and high school years, I was on a sedative medication that made it difficult to get up in the morning.

When Jeff was in grade two, I read a book on how to raise independent children. It suggested that whatever a child was able to do for himself, he should be encouraged to do. The book inspired me to train him to prepare his own egg and toast in the morning. When he called to me to say goodbye, I got up long enough to make sure he had eaten, packed his lunch, dressed properly and combed his hair. Then I returned to bed until I was able to truly wake up and start the day. This was our routine throughout his elementary school life. On the medication I was taking at the time, I could do no more.

Yet if I was a bad mother before school, I was a good mother at the end of the day. I made a point of being there when he arrived home, ready with a snack and time for talk at the kitchen table. At 3:30, he got my undivided attention.

I enrolled him in classes and sports activities, as most parents did. He went to soccer, skating and swimming classes, drama lessons and summer art classes. He was also in Boy Scouts. But I made a conscious effort not to over-extend him in organized programs. I wanted him to have time to do his own thing. He never forgot how to create his own projects and fun.

Starting in grade six, I took him to drum lessons and bought him a full set of drums. Drumming became an ever present noise in our house. He produced an unbelievable racket, causing me much stress. But I believed the drumming was a good release for him, especially important during his teens. I wanted him to continue. Eventually we arranged for him to have his practice time after school, giving us rest for the remainder of the day.

While Jeff was in high school, his friends felt welcome in our home. They often gathered at our place for band practice, to watch videos, make videos or play monopoly deep into the night. Jeff's friends became my friends.

Wes and I must have done something right because he always made a point of being home at dinnertime. He was disappointed if he was late and missed it. Sitting around the table provided opportunities for good conversation—something we all enjoyed.

I did the best I knew how as Jeff's mother, but I'm disappointed I didn't make more effort at helping him with his school work. He seemed to want independence from us in that respect. He did not welcome our help. Should I have pressed harder? Perhaps. Or might it have made things worse?

I did succeed in one major way. I am grateful I had the ability and inspiration to encourage him to be creative. Today, as a result, he has a life that is rich with many interests.

## Was Having a Bipolar Mom Harmful?

SOMETIMES I HEAR or read discussions on how children's lives are affected by parents with bipolar disorder. Some of these stories suggest that having such a mother or father causes hardship for the children or might even damage them in some way.

Sean Astin, son of Patty Duke, was interviewed by Reader's Digest in August 2004. His mother was famous, not only as an actress but also as someone who has bipolar disorder. He described some of her episodes. "There would be shrieking and slapping; she'd throw dishes or break toys. Once she went after me with a wire coat hanger."

Yet aside from the stormy periods and days locked in her bedroom in despair, she was a good mom, showering her children with love. "Ninety-nine percent of the time I had it good—I realize now," Astin said, "and the one percent that was painful made me appreciate the other 99 all the more....And while she tried to protect me from hardships she suffered, I'm a beneficiary of her wisdom. When something bad happened to me, I used it to fuel something good." I hope, to some extent, that might be true for my son as well.

Jeff told me that he remembers a lot of yelling and screaming. And my long periods of seclusion in the bedroom—even though he doesn't remember them—must have made for a depressing home atmosphere.

Although I had countless episodes of depression, mania and psychosis throughout his childhood, Jeff did not become aware that I had a mental illness until grade six or seven. Only then did he learn that my mood problems were the result of bipolar disorder. But I don't think he ever held it against me. In fact, when he became a teenager, there were times when he showed me a lot of understanding. Though I wasn't always at my best in those days, I don't think he was ashamed of me. Bringing his pals home so often indicates he wasn't.

When *Riding the Roller Coaster* was published, Jeff was in his mid-twenties. Although it contains vivid descriptions of my mental health struggles, he was not embarrassed. In fact, he seemed proud of me for writing the book. At the time it came out, he was working in a music and electronics business which also stocked books. Jeff made sure that my book was on the shelf. When I visited the store some time later, he made a point of introducing me to all his co-workers.

Jeff may have had problems because of my disorder, even ones he isn't aware of today. Looking back, I can see things I could have done better and things I did wrong. Jeff recently confessed that the only serious problem he had with me was around grade six when he felt overprotected. He wanted more independence and had even threatened to run away from home. Life would probably have been easier for him had I been a more balanced, more healthy mom. But I believe that, perhaps because of me, he has also learned to be an understanding and compassionate human being.

Motherhood was an important, joyous challenge for me, one I wouldn't have missed for the world. I love my son dearly; he helped make my life complete.

I asked Wes, "What kind of a mother was I? Did my illness affect my mothering very much?" I told him I wanted to know the truth. To my relief, he said, "You were a good mother. The only thing is that you were overprotective." And when I asked whether I yelled and screamed a lot, he said, "Not nearly as much as you think." This is good to know.

*Chapter 4*

# MY FAITH
# JOURNEY

## I Discover a Bible

WHEN I GAVE birth to Jeff, all ten pounds of him, I had a long, difficult time of it. After eighteen hours in labor, a caesarian section became necessary. I began suffering emotionally almost immediately. Soon psychosis took over.

My psychiatrist arranged for a private room. Here I waited to recover sufficiently physically before moving to the psychiatric ward. This new room was on a quiet, isolated ward, and nurses did not look in on me very often. Wes worked full-time and was only able to visit me for a while each evening. I spent many hours alone.

Whenever I was able, I went to the nursery to feed the baby and cuddle him, but not nearly often enough. Jeff's pediatrician came to me on a couple of occasions to explain how important it was for me to bond with my new son, to spend as much time as I could with him. I had very much wanted him and wanted to be a good mother, so I did my best. But he needed more than I was able to provide. I couldn't give Jeff my full attention when my mind was constantly occupied with delusional thoughts. To make matters worse, some of the staff in the nursery shunned me, treating me indifferently, making me feel unwelcome. (I'm sure I wasn't imagining this.)

The mental torture I went through at this time was of the worst kind. At night I stayed awake for hours, often not sleeping at all. All I could do was think rapid thoughts that did not reflect reality. To deal with my mind's vigorous activity, I began to write, hoping this would relieve some of the stress and might even prove helpful to someone one day. "If I have to suffer," I thought, "at least let all this be useful for something."

My ground-floor room looked out onto the main entrance of the hospital. Here stood the tall Christmas tree that was traditionally erected each holiday season. January had arrived, and it was time to remove it. As I watched the workmen digging around the tree and preparing to bring it down, my anxiety grew. The paranoia that had begun plaguing me made me think there was a bomb underneath, ready to explode. As the work progressed, the fear escalated until I panicked, rushing down the hall, trying to tell the staff of the imminent danger. But, try as I might, I couldn't speak intelligibly. My words were a muddle; I could not make sentences. My anxiety and agitation remained a mystery to the nurses.

But a revelation occurred in this room, impacting me deeply. In the drawer of my bedside table, I found a Gideon Bible.

With my request for no visitors except Wes, I had many lonely hours to fill. I began to read the New Testament, Psalms and Proverbs and found treasures there. I recognized truths in the verses and realized that the God I had learned about, but had not believed in, must be real. The book gave me new comfort. I felt that the authors knew, and were sympathetic to, what I was going through.

This was a more accessible Bible than the one I had used in my teens. At the front was a section listing where to find help for the problems you might be facing: what to read when you are afraid, desperate, distressed or troubled. Many topics in the list applied to me. I read voraciously, with a kind of hunger I had not experienced before.

One topic, "Where to find help when victimized," directed me to Hebrews 13:6: *The Lord is my helper, I will not be afraid. What will man do to me?"* I found an authoritative voice here, one I could trust. God became real to me. Though the paranoia did not disappear, my fears were temporarily soothed each time I read.

I found peace in John 14:27 when I read Christ's words, *"Peace I leave with you; my peace I give to you; not as the world gives do I give to you. Do not let your heart be troubled, nor let it be fearful."* To realize that God was looking after me gave me comfort.

For the first time in my life, God spoke to me through the Bible. I could see why so many had faith in God's power and love. My mental turmoil did not go away; I was not healed, only given relief while I was reading. Recovery would take much time and medical care, but with the help of this Bible, I found hope.

Seeds left in the ground over winter are aided in the germination process. After such a long time in the ground, their skin becomes roughened, allowing for better growth. In a similar way, during the trials I experienced at this time, when my heart was beaten and worn, I was finally ready to accept what the Bible was telling me.

God's Word kept me company, yet my mind continued working endlessly. I wrote down my overflowing thoughts in an effort to contain them. Many were reflections on what I had learned from the Bible.

When my psychiatrist came to visit, I asked him with the innocence of a child, "It wouldn't be such a bad thing to die, would it? I would be with God." I didn't by any means plan to take my life; I was only expressing a truth I had discovered. But my doctor misunderstood. He arranged for a young woman to sit with me every day until I moved to the psychiatric ward. I liked having her there.

We talked while she crocheted. My mind did not go off on tangents as much, and I was able to stay in the real world, able to keep a better perspective on things.

I copied some of my favorite verses out of the Bible and took them with me to the psychiatric ward. Eager to share a particularly valuable verse, I wrote it on a blackboard in the ward's lounge. This was the only thing written on the board for the week or two I remained there. I often wonder if anyone was helped by it.

Unfortunately, once I left the hospital and began adjusting to motherhood, I did not follow through on what I had learned in that hospital bed. For many years, I forgot this revelation. I went back to my old life, relying on my own strength, struggling and sometimes breaking. Thoughts about God and the Bible receded to the back of my mind. Not until fourteen years later, during another stormy period, did my spiritual hunger return. Only then did I begin to search for God in earnest.

# Before I Believed

WHEN I WAS three or four years old, I was doing something I shouldn't, and my mother warned me that I wouldn't go to heaven if I continued. I retorted, "I don't want to go to heaven anyway!" and meant it. In spite of my Christian upbringing, I had not learned to think of Jesus as someone I could love. Not with that long scratchy beard of his! Men with beards scared me, and I could not think of myself sitting in his lap and being happy about it. My mother, very angry, put me into a dark closet and left me there for what seemed like a long time. I cried bitterly, becoming evermore defiant. This rebelliousness was out of character for me. I was normally a good girl, an obedient girl.

My husband, Wes, was also raised in the church but left it when he was in his late teens, as I did. When we were a young couple, instead of going to church, we spent Sunday mornings enjoying the outdoors. With our cameras, we recorded the beauty of creation, marveling at how light could transform a simple land-scape, lying flat on our stomachs to photograph delicate wildflow-ers. Smugly I thought to myself, "Isn't this a more apt way to wor-ship than being confined to a stuffy church?" I needed to rationalize not being in church, never able to get over the guilt I harbored for rejecting my family's faith.

Yet there were sleepless nights when I struggled to find an-swers to what made the natural world work so perfectly. After much thinking, I created a definition of God that I could live with: 'the force that drives nature.' Neat and simple. That relieved my guilt somewhat. But the God I had made up was not someone I could place my confidence in, or go to when I was in need, or thank for all that was good in my life. I had to continue battling my illness on my own, trusting my dubious willpower.

My life was full with photography, camera club and commu-nity activities. I freelanced for a community newspaper for a while. Although the remuneration was low, the satisfaction was immense. I doubt whether anyone without manic depressive tendencies would have approached the job with such enthusiasm. I liked hav-ing photographs published that expressed the way I felt about life. I liked telling stories I thought were important.

Yet, in spite of my rich life, in spite of the joy of my photogra-phy, even the awards and gallery showings, I found the lines of an old Peggy Lee song creeping into my head: "Is that all there is? Is that all there is?" And the question haunting me was the one Rick Warren poses on the cover of his book, *The Purpose Driven Life*: "What on earth am I here for?"

## I Recognize My Need

AT A PARTICULARLY difficult time in my life, a time of stress, over-whelming emotion and a creative high that made coping difficult, I decided to take another look at the God I had rejected. No one urged me to do this; the resolve came from within. I think of it as

God tapping me on the shoulder, reminding me of what I had read in the Gideon Bible many years earlier: *"Here I am! I stand at the door and knock. If anyone hears my voice and opens the door, I will come in and eat with him, and he with me."* (Revelations 3:20) Jesus was knocking on my door.

Two things convinced me to break down the wall I had built up against God. First was my mental health. I needed help with my battles, and I wondered whether God could really help me in the way people said God could. Second was my photography. The stories my pictures were telling had become truly special. I suspected there was something else at work here. How could this possibly be my work alone? Could this be God's guiding hand? In a remarkable way, God gradually showed himself to me through my photographs.

## A Photograph Reveals God's Love for Me

I HAD SPENT two years doing photography part-time for the community newspaper when I came up with the idea for a project. At the school my son attended, physically and mentally challenged children had been integrated with healthy ones. I noticed how some of the able-bodied students went out of their way to befriend those with disabilities. My neighbor even told me how one young girl drew pictures and wrote poems for one of them on a regular basis.

With permission of the school board, the principal and parents, I spent several lunch hours in the playground documenting the relationships among the children. I had to carry out my work with care, not letting the children suspect why I was taking pictures. Although most news photographs are set up, the pictures I was looking for had to be candid and truthful—authentic expressions of love.

Towards the end of my third lunch hour, I took a break to chat with the principal. That's when the moment I had been looking for came. A few feet away, a young girl bent over a boy in a wheelchair.

With an expression of love, she gave full attention to the boy. The cerebral-palsied child could only make gurgling sounds. This did not stop the two from communicating. The girl repeated similar sounds back to him, and in this way they "talked." Real words were not needed to express their friendship. After a while, she straightened up, squeezed his hand and smiled down at him with a look of encouragement before running off to play with other friends.

Fortunately, my camera was ready. I stopped my conversation mid-sentence and moved forward a few steps, quickly capturing several frames of this intimate exchange. I hadn't dreamed I would be able to capture images so exquisite or meaningful! When I developed the pictures and saw they had turned out well, I was ecstatic. The school board used them in a newsletter to city residents, and the newspaper used some others taken during those days. Both publications ran stories with the photos.

That series of pictures did something to me. For a long time I didn't know what it was.

In the months following, I gave a number of presentations about my work to groups of photographers. As I did so, I discussed my enlarged prints, each one in turn, explaining why I took the picture and what it meant to me. This was easy. I was never at a loss for words when talking about my pictures. But each time I came to the images of the girl and boy in the schoolyard, I couldn't speak. Instead, tears welled up in my eyes, and I was left mumbling something unintelligible.

Around this time, I began to search for God. I was doing a lot of photography that surprised and overwhelmed me. This elevated me into a manic state. I had trouble staying together. My mind and body could not find rest. I had survived many periods of mental anguish, but this time I wished for more help than medications and personal willpower could offer. I was exhausted and wanted very much to let go instead of holding on.

I gradually decided to re-evaluate my resistance to God. Was there something to this Christian faith after all? Wouldn't it be wonderful if it were all true! I wanted to find out. I needed the kind of help they said God could give. I needed an end to the turmoil in my head. I wanted peace.

What made me so interested in discovering expressions of love in that playground? Why did those pictures move me so? I can now see that through those pictures and others I took around that time, Christ revealed himself to me. He was knocking on my door. In that girl's face, I found the love of Jesus. And subconsciously I saw myself as the child in the wheelchair.

Today I realize I don't make my photographs solely by my own efforts. When I seek God daily with an open and sincere heart, God's spirit is present in all my creative work.

# My Search

FINDING GOD did not happen overnight. And believing in Jesus as my Savior took even longer. A wall of defiance such as the one I had built up over the years cannot be torn down overnight. Even after it's down, clearing away the rubble takes time. The name of Jesus was so foreign to my lips that it took some time before I dared to utter it. I even felt awkward saying the word "Bible." It was awhile before I could say these words comfortably without feeling self-conscious.

Strangely enough, I did not go to church when I began to search for God. Church was not a place I was ready for. I called a photographer acquaintance in another city, a retired minister I didn't know well, and asked him if he could tell me more about God. But he lived too far away, and we had no opportunity to get together.

Then I began to look in the public library for something that might help me. I found a few books, but they only added to my confusion. For a long time, I didn't know what I was looking for or what I needed. Where to go from here?

All those years from toddler to teen, I had heard the Bible stories and learned about Jesus, but it was as though I hadn't been there. It was all new to me now. I had to learn everything again, from the ground up. But now my heart was open enough to absorb and accept, to learn about his love for me. An incident at a family get-together at my in-laws' home shows just how hungry I was.

Wes's cousin, was having a serious discussion with our brother-in-law, Henry. This cousin's mother had recently died, and he was in a similar position to mine—he also wanted to learn about the Christian faith. He asked Henry one question after another. I very much wanted to join them because I, too, needed answers. But I was at the dining room table playing a game. How I wanted to listen in, and how I struggled to follow what they were saying! Concentration on the game became almost impossible. I was drawn like a magnet to the discussion.

If I had had the chance to leave the game and enter into the conversation, would I have? Would I have been willing to swallow my pride and, with the family there to witness it, finally admit that I had been wrong in denying my faith? I will never forget the passionate longing I experienced that afternoon. God was already a reality for me, the promise of a better life. God knocked and I was ready to listen.

# Church

A COUPLE OF friends I respected attended the United Church of Canada. If they were going to church, it must be OK, I thought. I decided to try it. But before I did, I asked one of them, "Is this the kind of church where people get saved, like in the evangelical churches?" I did not want to go to a church that was driven by emotional spirituality. The whole concept of "being saved" reminded me too much of the church of my youth. Sharon replied, "I think maybe 10—20% of them would call themselves born again." That suited me fine. But I wondered what made me so afraid of "feeling" the presence of God. Why was I afraid of sharing my testimony with others?

I decided to go the next Sunday. "But," my friend said, "this is going to be a different kind of service, not our usual kind. It's Easter, and there will be a performance of the Easter story by a group of children." What a coincidence! I hadn't remembered it was Easter.

The children's joyful acting and singing touched me deeply. As I sat next to Sharon, I could not contain my tears; I wept uncontrollably. I, a person who had been afraid of emotion in church, was the most emotional worshiper that day. We sat near the front of the sanctuary, allowing me no opportunity to walk out gracefully. Such a wonderful, upbeat program, yet I sobbed as though someone had died! I didn't know why. Nevertheless, I went back the next week, and for the next fourteen years.

The United Church was very different from the Baptist Church I had been accustomed to. The service was formal, with prayers read from the bulletin. I came to like it. The hymns filled me with inspiration and led me on my journey of faith. I was eager to learn and joined a Bible study group at the first opportunity. I soon found out how archaic my old Bible was. No one used the King James version anymore. The church had changed. More friendly translations had been published.

For the first time since my youth, I heard the Bible stories. I learned about Jesus and his love for me. But now the message penetrated and stayed with me. My heart had become softened and ready to absorb.

Not until some time later did I realize I had been born on an Easter Sunday morning—in April 1946.

# I Begin my Walk with Jesus

THE CHURCH I had chosen did not have occasions during the services when attendees were publicly led to Christ. That was one of the reasons I had decided to go there. I felt safer that way. No one had to know my private business. I didn't have to endure the embarrassment of praying with someone. My salvation came to me in the quiet privacy of my bedroom.

I didn't know what God required of a follower of Christ: to ask for forgiveness of my sins; to accept that Jesus died for me and rose again; to consciously invite him into my life. Gradually I learned from sermons and the Bible. Gradually Jesus became a part of my life.

My prayers were, and still are, a haphazard array of disconnected thoughts directed to God. But one prayer, which held a lot of meaning for me, was a complete request. I often began the day praying, "Please, God, fill my heart with your love and help me share it with others." I wasn't planning on converting my friends; I just wanted to love others the way Jesus shows his love in the Bible. I wanted to do what he tells us: love my neighbors, everyone I might meet. This made a lot of sense to me.

When I started these prayers, I was immediately flooded with peace, warmth and joy. Encouraged, I returned to this prayer many times, and, without any further conscious effort, a change came over me. I became friendlier. My shy nature gave way to a more outgoing one. I stopped losing my temper with my family and became more patient and accepting. These new qualities were what Paul, in Galatians 5:22–23, calls the fruit of the Spirit. They grew in me simply by asking Jesus to fill me with his love. Jesus said, *"Ask and it will be given to you; seek and you will find; knock and the door will be opened to you."* (Matthew 7:7) How true that has been for me!

But my conversion was not yet complete. In the months that followed, I asked God to forgive my sins, and I expressed my belief in Jesus as my Savior. My journey of faith began with uncertainty, without a clear roadmap. I eventually learned there are never obvious directions to follow. As long as I trust, God will lead me and show me the way. This is what God does.

At first I didn't tell anyone of my spiritual rebirth, especially not my family. I felt guilty about that, but I needed time. I did not obey Christ's admonition to *"Go home to your family and tell them how much the Lord has done for you, and how he has had mercy on you."* (Mark 5:19) Was it that old defiant me not wanting to admit I had given in? Or was I afraid of the emotions that might be lavished upon me? I did not understand what Paul wrote in Romans 10:10 (NLT): *"...it is by believing in your heart that you are made right with God, and it is by confessing with your mouth that you are saved."*

Only gradually did I begin to share my new faith, first with my Bible study class. In the safety of this group of women I had come to know well, I took many opportunities to witness. I especially liked to share, often out of the blue, how much Christ's words in Matthew 11 had meant to me: *"Come to me, all you who are weary and burdened and I will give you rest...."* Most of the women grew up believing in God; they had not had a conversion experience. They could not identify with my description of finding Christ for the first time.

I finally invited my family to join me in my new life of faith when I was baptized. My parents, my sister Ann and her husband were part of the celebration. An adult baptism was rather rare in this church. The pastor dipped his fingers in the holy water, touched my forehead and asked me to repeat my profession of faith after him.

In later years, when I began attending the evangelical Brentwood Park Alliance Church, I discovered what my baptism could have been—more of a celebration, with an opportunity to tell my story. Today I wish I had had the chance to talk about what God had done for me and what God means to me. But would I have been ready for that back then? Maybe not.

Nevertheless, a new, more meaningful life had begun. I stopped creating photographs of sad children and empty playgrounds in fog-shrouded parks. I no longer felt such a great need to work for my own benefit, for personal recognition or material wealth. Although I wasn't sure what I would do, I wanted my energies to go into helping others.

And I continue to change.

# A New Freedom

YEARS AGO I knew a little boy I'll call Robbie. His mom was easygoing and felt that a child would do fine on his own. She was confident he would learn right from wrong without interference from his parents so long as they made sure he didn't do any damage or hurt anyone. This, she thought, would encourage independence. She believed that parents who worried too much about their children were overprotective. In fact, she didn't know how to set limits. She confided in me, "I don't really know what's wrong and what's right."

One day, when our family was visiting theirs, Robbie proudly announced to my son, "My mom is going to give us rules. We will have special times when we can watch TV and all kinds of things like that." He delighted in having some guidelines and in the attention his mother was suddenly paying to what he did and did not do. This unusual reaction from a child made a big impression on me. It showed how much children need rules and how lost they become without them. His mom's new rules made Robbie feel that she cared for him enough to help him understand what was good for him.

The same holds true for adults. Robbie's relief and happiness in the face of his new rules parallels what happened to me when I began to follow Christ. I found out how good it is to have guidelines for my day-to-day life. I wanted to hear and please God because I knew God loved me, as parents love their children. God wanted what was best for me. I learned Jesus' most important commandment, summed up in two parts: *"Love the Lord your God with all your heart and with all your soul and with all your mind."* and *"Love your neighbor as yourself."* (Matthew 22:37, 38)

No longer did I have to struggle blindly to find my way. Paradoxically, obedience to God liberated me. I was released from the desire to live according to the world's ideals: the idols of materialism, ambition, power and approval from others. I discovered that I was happiest when I worked for God instead of for my own selfish gains. As Paul wrote in his letter, *"...you have been called to live in freedom—not freedom to satisfy your sinful nature, but freedom to serve one another in love."* (Galatians 5:13) Quite the opposite of a burden! Earnestly seeking to please God led to a joyful, meaningful way of living.

I was freed when I tore down the wall of resistance, opened my heart and submitted to God. I felt much as Robbie did when his mom helped him know what was best for him. I now have Someone I can trust to be my guide, Someone who will help me distinguish right from wrong, Someone who cares about what happens to me. God forgave my sins and gave me freedom from guilt.

Dietrich Bonhoeffer wrote: "The command of Jesus is hard, unutterably hard, for those who try to resist it. But for those who willingly submit, the yoke is easy, and the burden is light."[1] The "yoke" of serving God has proven easy, as Christ promised. It is a "burden" I welcome. This yoke is the yoke of a loving parent for me, his child.

# New Courage

AFTER I BEGAN following Christ, I started educating others about mental health issues. I wrote articles and a book about what it is like to live with bipolar disorder. I expressed my anger about the unfair stigma attached to the disorder. God helped me feel good about myself and gave me the courage to speak up. I, the quiet and shy young girl who had been afraid to open her mouth in class, became an activist. God wanted this for me because the urge to speak out and educate the public never leaves me. Sometimes I get sidetracked, but I always come back to this purpose I have found for my life. God has given me gifts suited to this work, and I receive great satisfaction from them. My life is full, and I'm happy knowing I'm doing something worthwhile—God's work.

I still struggle with my disorder more often than I would like. In all likelihood, I always will. But, thanks to God and the support of those who love me, including a wonderful group of Christian friends, my mental health is better than it was before I became a believer. I still have bipolar disorder; that won't go away. But I know that *"...my hope comes from him. He alone is my rock and my salvation; he is my fortress..."* (Psalm 62:5–6)

Now, I look upon my difficult mood swings as something I can ultimately use for good. How can I speak out for people with mood disorders if I have forgotten what they are like? This book is a product of those mood swings, of the highs and the lows; it is a product of hard times.

## I Was Blind, But Now I See

I HAVE OFTEN wondered why it took me so long to know God and understand what the Bible was trying to tell me. During my childhood and teens, I lived in a Christian home and attended Sunday school. Yet nothing had penetrated. I had always done my best to be the kind of person my parents wanted me to be: quiet, respectful, doing my best at school. I had been submissive towards both my parents and others. Yet I did not submit to God. Except for the time as a preschooler when I said I didn't want to go to heaven, I can't remember any open denial. But I harbored a mild coolness and non-acceptance.

Why did I take so long to find God?

The hymn Amazing Grace, written by John Newton, has a special meaning for me. It's not surprising. Many people feel the same way. The words are a clear expression of what happened to me:

*"I once was lost, but now am found;*
*Was blind, but now I see."*

Awhile ago the words, *"I was blind, but now I see,"* kept repeating themselves in my mind. I had a lot in common with the man quoted in John 9 who had been blind from birth and living in darkness until Jesus healed him.

I was also "blind" from birth, blind to understanding who Jesus was and what he could do for me. I had heard the words, but they were only words. I learned about him but did not get to know him. Finally, when I reached the age of forty-two, God opened my eyes.

But why did God take so long?

On re-reading the story, I discovered a possible answer to my question. When the disciples asked, *"who sinned, this man or his parents, that he was born blind?"* Jesus explained how no one was to blame: He said *"...this happened so that the work of God might be displayed in his life."* (John 9:2–3) Knowing what it means to be blind gave the man a greater appreciation for his sight and for what Jesus had done for him. He became a strong, fearless witness for Christ, even though it meant being thrown out of the Synagogue.

In the same way, because of my years of not recognizing him, Jesus is more precious to me than he might have been had I known him all along. The peace and joy I have found by placing my trust in him has been healing. He has given me a reason for living. He has given me hope during difficult times. I sense his love deeply.

The changes others now see in me bear witness to what God can do. His touch can perform miracles. My new ability to see, so late in life, has given me a passion to obey God and use the gifts God has given me to serve. All those years of darkness have helped me appreciate God's grace.

# Fruits of the Spirit

*"Therefore, as God's chosen people, holy and dearly loved, clothe your-selves with compassion, kindness, humility, gentleness and patience. Bear with each other and forgive whatever grievances you may have against one another. Forgive as the Lord forgave you." (Colossians 3:12–13)*

I BELIEVE THAT, while I was still a child, God gave me some of the qualities that Paul describes here in Colossians. My parents showered me with Christian love, encouraging me to be kind, gentle and patient. And, as I have said many times in my story, my compassion for others grew as I struggled with my many mood swings.

I was very shy and did not think much of myself. I seem to have been born with humility. Through my adult years, however, I had to strive to "clothe" myself with less pride. I was proud of my photographs and felt great temptation, whenever someone visited, to show off my work. I tried not to do that and still do at times, though I'm better able to control myself now.

When I became a Christian, I learned to forgive people who hurt me. When a friend comes out with a barrage of swear words, I wince. But I've learned to look past this and see what's in his heart. I've learned not to be too judgmental.

One of the most difficult individuals to forgive has been me. My strong moods have caused me to make numerous blunders. I have said stupid things without thinking. Often it's not until hours or days later that I realize what I've said. I become embarrassed, worried sick about how others took my words. I awake in the middle of the night thinking about what I did, kicking myself. It's so hard to forgive myself.

On the other hand, being aware of all the mistakes I've made helps me forgive others when *they* make mistakes. I try to put myself in their shoes. We are all human, and no human is perfect. I try to love no matter what, as well as I'm able. I try to forgive, as God forgives me.

In recent years, I've become able to speak more freely to others, without fear of saying the wrong thing. It's easier to be myself. I've learned to backtrack and apologize when I think I've hurt a friend. I feel much better when my friend realizes I didn't want to hurt her. It's best to be honest about my behavior.

I have begun spending more time each morning reading my Bible and praying. I'm walking closer to God. The payoff? I seem to be getting myself into less hot water. I don't say as many hurtful or embarrassing things. I'm more confident and open in showing my love towards those around me. I don't have to kick myself quite so often.

# I Don't Believe in *If* Anymore

WITH THE GREATEST determination, I used to cling to what was left of my mind's composure. I felt as though I were hanging from the edge of a high rooftop, white-knuckled, panicky with fear. How long can I hold on like this? Can I maintain my strength? What will happen if I let go? Exhaustion overwhelmed me. Far below was the hard ground and no one to catch me if I fell.

But I did fall—quite often. These experiences were devastating and difficult to recover from. The support I received from family, friends and my doctor was helpful, but I was alone in the battle.

Rudyard Kipling's poem *If* was like a bible to me during many years of my illness. I described in *Riding the Roller Coaster* how meaningful this poem became, how I patterned my life after its good counsel, how I carried it with me for many years. It encouraged me to become a productive and responsible person. I still think highly of the poem and try to go along with most of its advice. I follow through on my dreams, don't worry about what others say and try as much as possible to "*...fill the unforgiving minute* *with sixty seconds' worth of distance run."* But I no longer listen to the challenge Kipling leaves us with these words:

> *If you can force your heart and nerve and sinew*
> *To serve your turn long after they are gone,*
> *And so hold on when there is nothing in you*
> *Except the Will, which says to them, "Hold on!"*

For twenty-three years, I tried to live out those lines when I was in crisis. I tried with my best willpower to survive the mental turmoil that overtook me. I was determined to be strong, hanging on to whatever I could, but not finding much of substance. Those were times of anxiety and fear.

Coping with crisis finally changed for the better when I could no longer deny that God is real. I realized I didn't have to depend on myself alone. I could relax my grip and trust in someone much stronger than me.

The faith I learned to have in a God who loves me too much to let me go helps me cope better with stress. Extreme difficulties no longer develop as often. Sometimes I still have a fear of falling, and for good reason. But today I have a Bible that tells me, *"Don't be afraid, for I am with you. Do not be dismayed, for I am your God. I will strengthen you. I will help you. I will uphold you with my victorious right hand."* (Isaiah 41:10, NLT) Remembering this gives me comfort when I need it. I am not as afraid anymore.

Challenging periods will always be part of my life. There will be times when I'll have trouble. I may even fall. But I know that when I do, there will be someone there to catch me and stay with me as I recover. I'll never be alone again.

Hanging on the wall across from my bed is a photograph of a child's small hand resting comfortably on her father's big hand. Underneath are the words from Proverbs 3:5, *"Trust in the Lord with all your heart and lean not on your own understanding."* During tough times, I look at that photograph and feel a sense of peace. No longer is there a need for white-knuckled fists, no longer a need to rely on my own inadequate strength.

## Love Drives Out Fear

TO "FEAR" GOD, as the Bible says in many places, means to be in awe of God. It means to be fully aware of what God has created, to appreciate what God does for us, to sense how great and loving God is. When we fear God, we don't need to fear anything else. Yet in the midst of deep depression, mania or psychosis, this is not always possible.

In his letter, John said, *"There is no fear in love. But perfect love drives out fear."* (1 John 4:18) When things are at their worst, I receive momentary comfort from those words. But hanging on to that knowledge is difficult. As I move through the day, the fear returns.

I try my hardest to cling to God's words, *"Never will I leave you; never will I forsake you."* (Hebrews 13:5) When I'm feeling alone in my struggles, they offer relief. I'm better able to trust in my ability to be well. I'm better able to survive the mood upheavals. I can then think: people can't hurt me, death can't hurt me, why be afraid? Though I suffer, I know that God is ultimately in control; God will eventually help something good come out of the bad.

I lose some of my anxiety when I know my Christian friends are thinking of me and praying for me. When they express their love for me, I feel God's love. When they encourage me, I feel God's encouragement. I feel cared for. There is no need to fear.

## I Changed

GOD HAS GRADUALLY changed me from the inside out. My love for God and others began buried deep within. I did not know how to express it. With God's help, the love gradually worked its way out from the center until I was able to give it free expression.

Encouraged by the freedom I found in Christ, I learned how to be myself with others. Because of the trust I put in God, I was re-made into someone who knew how to be more loving. I became less judgmental and more forgiving.

When I think of the place of rest I've found, I recall the photographs I made at the school playground—of the love on the girl's face I had been blessed to capture. I thank God for leading me there, for putting it in my heart to look for Jesus, for helping me drop the barrier I had built up against him. Through God's work in me, I was able to accept Jesus into my heart and allow him to love me.

I feel more secure, more confident, more able to be well. I changed—and I continue changing.

## God, My Constant

MY FAITH HAS been firm for a long time, thank God. I know God is there, even when I feel abandoned. God is always watching over me. God is a constant.

I know God is there in the dark times and in the bright times; in my joy and in my sorrow; in the pain of illness and in my wellness; in my loneliness and in my times with friends. God is in my struggles and in my peace. Jesus is my most trustworthy friend. He is the only one who fully understands. When I suffer, he suffers with me. He loves me, no matter what.

# PART THREE:
## COPING

*Chapter 5*

# COPING WITH THE UPS AND DOWNS

*Depression?*

*Have I done it? Have I hit the low Dr. Long thought possible, the one I proudly and confidently said could never happen?*

*My body feels heavy, and I don't want to move off this bed. I doze, enjoying the peace I had yearned for so long. Yes, nice in a way, but I know in my heart I mustn't give in to this.*

*But surely this feeling isn't here to stay! This can't be! Not me! I've been well and without depression for such a long time. I felt invincible. But now? With 150,000 dead in the Asia tsunami and me so lucky and safe? How could depression be possible for someone like me?*

*I think of my new church friends, the women I'm growing to love so much. I wish for their prayers; I know prayer would help. But I feel too proud to ask. I'm supposed to be a strong person, someone who wrote a book about coping with such things.*

*What are they going to think when they find out I'm in trouble and in need? And, with Wes out of town? Alone. What can they possibly do for me? I don't want to burden them.*

## Willpower and Coping Skills: Never Enough

IT IS BECOMING clear to me that I can't avoid occasional instability. When I have a cold, I can try to get rid of it with vitamin C and echinacea, rest and hot drinks. Usually I just have to be patient and let it run its course.

Avoiding and overcoming depression and mania present similar challenges. I can do all the right things to stay balanced, but I will never be able to completely avoid falling into depression or rising to mania. They are a natural part of my makeup. God can help me cope; I can trust God to be there for me, but this mood disorder will always be part of me. And when symptoms arise, usually all I can do is be patient and let them run their course.

What I need most for my well-being is medication. In the same way a person with diabetes needs insulin, I need medication to stay stable. Even when I faithfully follow doctor's orders and take my pills, there are times when they are not enough. Sometimes my treatment regime needs adjusting; sometimes I need a different cocktail of medications.

I've learned helpful ways of coping when symptoms appear. They are never perfect, yet sometimes they lessen the pain. During severe depressions, these strategies might be next to impossible to employ and might not make a dent in my mood. Yet I must always try to do my best.

## Getting Medical Help

FEAR IS HARD to avoid when depression sets in. I try not to push the panic button too quickly. Occasional down-days can happen, but a full-blown depression might not come at all. Running to the doctor and asking for medication too quickly means I am anxious, and that tends to worsen my negative mood. Yet neither should I linger in this state too long before getting professional help.

At the beginning of depression, my thoughts turn inward. I become wrapped up in myself, trying to identify what is happening. I know what depression can do to me and, naturally, I fear it. But I must fight this fear. The most healing thing I can do is turn my attention away from myself and get busy on physical activities, anything to keep me from falling into the trap of sitting in solitary thought for long periods.

At times my mind is so busy I begin to feel detached from my surroundings. I become like a child, not aware of what's going on around me. I have to take special care walking through parking lots or crossing streets.

To guard against being consumed by my endless thinking, I go out with other people and engage in the world around me. Keeping my social life active is important. Talking with others and hearing about what's happening in their lives keeps me in perspective and gives me a lift. I try to visit someone each day, either in person or by phone.

A trip to the mall and a treat of a cinnamon bun and coffee give me a boost. Sometimes I buy a small piece of clothing. I don't need to spend much; even shopping at a thrift store is satisfying. I try to focus on things outside myself and carry on as normally as possible—not as easy as it sounds.

When my bed is the most comfortable place to be—when I want to hide from the world—I can't find the energy to meet my commitments no matter how much I want to. Even the simplest tasks seem complex to me.

I try to look after my physical well-being by exercising or going for walks. Moving my body helps clear my brain. Even if my appetite is poor, I try to eat regularly. I do simple activities, things I can manage, work or play that will give me some satisfaction.

Although I usually don't have the time or patience to iron clothes, at times like these, when I'm struggling with mild depression, ironing is good therapy. Music helps me focus. Knowing we're going to have fresh clothes in the closet feels good. On the rare occasion when I reach the bottom of the stack, I'm delighted to find clothes I had forgotten. That boosts my spirit!

If I haven't improved after a week or so, I know I need to see my doctor. Allowing more time to go by is not an option. Getting professional help is no longer an expression of fear or anxiety; it makes good sense. The longer I wait to go on an antidepressant, the more difficult it will be to extract myself from the grips of this mood.

# Coping with Depression

I COPE BETTER with my depression if I temporarily lower my expectations for myself. I give myself permission to be more laid back. Instead of forcing myself to do what I "should" be doing, I look for something I can manage easily. I do things that give me enjoyment or satisfaction. I reduce my workload to make it fit within the limitations of my body and mind.

Once, I volunteered for a little job for the church folding pamphlets. There was no pressure, and I was able to work in the comfort of my own kitchen. I welcomed this opportunity to do something uncomplicated but helpful. As I played my favorite music, I slowly worked at it. Accomplishing this felt much better than spending the day in front of the television or in bed.

When chores become too difficult for me, I ask Wes for help. I'm encouraged when he helps me wash a stack of dishes. I cook simpler dinners with fewer ingredients and take shortcuts, buying frozen, ready-to-heat meals. I reschedule whatever commitments I can afford to put on hold.

My friend, Nan Dickie, author of *A Map for the Journey: Living Meaningfully with Recurring Depression*, told me, "Follow routine as well as you can. But you've got to understand early when depression threatens and respond appropriately by being kind to yourself. Let go of unimportant tasks that are difficult. Try to do what truly needs to be done."

Much of the pressure I feel from my load of commitments is unnecessary. It comes from worry rather than from what I actually have to do. When I get organized and make a list, I realize I don't have as big a load as I thought; everything is achievable.

When I battle this darkness, becoming anxious and stressed, reaching out to God helps me find peace. I take to heart what the apostle Paul wrote in Romans 8:38–39: *"For I am convinced that neither death nor life, neither angels nor demons, neither the present nor the future, nor any powers, neither height nor depth, nor anything else in all creation, will be able to separate us from the love of God that is in Christ Jesus our Lord."* God loves me and takes care of me; I need not be afraid.

# Taking Action

*"Then the Lord said to Moses, 'Why are you crying out to me? Tell the people to get moving!'" (Exodus 14:15)*

GOOD MEDICINES, those from my earthly doctor and from my heavenly Healer, are important. But a lot is up to me.

I cannot overcome my emotional problems by lying in bed. I could sit, read my Bible and pray all day when I'm battling the beginnings of depression. But I've learned that if I don't get up and do something, my recovery will be greatly impaired.

Twenty-one days before Christmas and after weeks of high activity, my concerned husband said to me, "You've been whirling around like a tornado!" He knew what might happen, and he was right. Depression threatened once again. Even with a positive mood and upbeat thoughts, my body was tired. I sat for long periods and had great trouble getting up. Occasionally I felt tears welling up. I wasn't sad, only exhausted and stressed from the hectic activity. Thanks to forty years of dealing with this disorder, I have learned a few things—I immediately planned for action.

# Making Adjustments

FOR MANY YEARS I have ended each day by making a list of things I want to accomplish the next day. This ensures I do what needs to be done. I waste less time in the morning wondering how I should use the day. This time when depression threatened, I lightened the load by writing fewer items in my day-timer for the next several days. I included plans for frequent get-togethers with friends, and I made sure the gym was in my schedule.

Cooking has been my hobby during my entire thirty-seven years of marriage. I enjoy trying out new recipes and receiving a surprise when I taste them. It is also good therapy for lows and highs. During this period, as I found depression creeping up on me, I decided to bake a simple cake.

As I listened to my favorite Yanni CD, I found and measured each ingredient. I'm not always so organized, but working slowly and methodically helped. Getting off the bed and into the kitchen had been difficult, but once started, the work became easier. I even began to enjoy myself. I felt stronger and recovered a sense of control. I put my creation in the oven, encouraged, knowing I had accomplished something.

Coping with depression is not as easy as baking a cake. When I'm depressed, I have a hard time thinking of things I might do to lift me out of that mood. I have no energy or desire to do anything. All I want is to go to bed and vegetate or sleep. As one day follows another without accomplishment, I begin to feel ugly and unworthy.

I seek out my friends, but all I can do is complain. I feel guilty for once again burdening those who support me. What can they possibly do to help? I need to know they are there for me, yet I feel ashamed to be seen this way.

I know how important it is to be around people, so I invited a couple of dear friends over for afternoon coffee and cake. In the morning, I tidied the house. Knowing that company was coming gave me an incentive to clean up. I had a purpose for the day. Although I was still subdued, I didn't feel quite as drawn to spending time in bed as I had been. The day was good. My spirit received a boost.

The next day was also promising. "Maybe I've turned the corner," I thought. But a couple of good days did not mean I was out of the woods. A few days later, I was down again.

That one day with my friends was helpful. But I have to focus on a positive activity every day. If I am to prevent my depression from deepening, I need to make plans for a fulfilling day every evening before going to bed.

# Midnight Anxiety

*Why do I awake in the middle of the night, feeling fearful and anxious? As I write this, my days have been positive, energetic and balanced. Not a hint of problems. But when the world is dark and still, I feel abandoned and experience the worst of times. Are they caused by the "dark forces of evil" so many talk about? Is it Satan?*

*When I awake with this anxiety, I write or pray. The feeling then disappears. I lay my head back on the pillow and sleep once more. But I ask myself, "Why? Why the good, happy, wholesome days and the fears at night?"*

*My doctor told me that what happens at night is the clearest indication of where I am psychologically. "Psychologically," he says. "Spiritually," some church friends would say. But do I really need to understand? All I know, and what is most important to me, is that turning to God helps.*

*Solomon wrote, "Trust in the Lord with all your heart and lean not on your own understanding." (Proverbs 3:5)*

*Reading this gives me comfort. I try to pray and trust in God and not lean on my own understanding or on the exact reason why these anxieties come.*

*I decide to let go of the puzzle. I decide to hand it over to God. Peace of mind returns, and I settle back to sleep.*

*In the morning, I check the list of plans I made for myself the day before. As I look forward to these promises for work, play and time with friends, fears and crying are forgotten. I face the day afresh, with vigor and gladness. I remember how good life actually is.*

*"...weeping may remain for a night, but rejoicing comes in the morning." (Psalm 30:5b)*

## Worry, My Worst Enemy

*"Do not be anxious about anything, but in everything, by prayer and petition, with thanksgiving, present your requests to God. And the peace of God, which transcends all understanding, will guard your hearts and your minds in Christ Jesus." (Philippians 4:6–7)*

WORRY HAS BEEN one of the worst obstacles to my wellness. Worry affects my ability to trust God; it affects my ability to function. I've found that worry can, all by itself, make me sick.

My moods often cause me to worry. A negative, depressed mood prevents me from being realistic. I exaggerate the severity of a problem and am not able to perceive how things truly are.

But although worry is unhealthy, I've found concern is quite a different thing. Concern can be useful and healthy if I use it correctly. The difference is this:

When I worry, my mind moves in an endless cycle of negative thinking. I'm like the old men I saw in Greece, constantly twirling their worry beads in an effort to overcome stress and anxiety. All my problems, my friends' and the world's, travel round and round in my mind. They're stuck there. I don't reach conclusions. My mind seizes up and I become depressed.

When I'm concerned about something, I actively search for solutions. My attitude is positive, not negative. I prayerfully plan how I can best remove the obstacles I face and move ahead with a hopeful spirit and sense of purpose. I trust God to lead me. I feel alive.

Actively dealing with my concerns motivates me; worry immobilizes me.

## Trust During Rough Times

DEPRESSION CAN BE a debilitating, torturous experience. During such times, I have to work hard to maintain my trust in God. I try not to be anxious but to relax and let God do his work in me and care for me. But it's difficult not to be afraid; it's natural to be afraid.

As my negative thinking takes over, I begin to doubt my ability to complete the projects I'm working on. I fear that friends no longer care about me and won't be there for me. I fear my depression will deepen and I might stop functioning altogether. I can't see how I could ever be cheerful again.

Philip Yancey, in his book, *Where is God When it Hurts?* explains how "fear is the universal response to suffering. And yet beyond a doubt it is also the single greatest 'enemy of recovery.'"[2] Fear is part of the extreme moods I go through, especially psychosis. The more I give in to fear, the worse my illness becomes. It is important to do all I can to escape it. The best way is to turn to God and trust in God. But it's hard.

David, the psalmist, fought similar battles. I need to pray along with him, *"When I am afraid, I will trust in you. In God, whose word I praise, in God, I trust; I will not be afraid."* (Psalm 56:3–4)

Since the dramatic change in my life when I began to follow Christ, my faith in God has remained steadfast. No matter how bad things become, I know God is there. But belief in God and trusting God are two different things. Trusting means relying on someone, having confidence in God's power to help me. I cannot always do this. I have to work at it, over and over again. I have to remind myself to turn to God when things are bad. Even when it seems useless to do so, I need to read my Bible and pray.

A habit I developed a few years ago has stood me in good stead—taking at least an hour of quiet time each morning. I start each day with Bible reading, prayer and journaling. These times do much to comfort and strengthen me, whether I'm excessively up or excessively down. Though my prayers are often awkward, though the words come slowly and with great effort, they help keep my focus on God. They help me stay close to God.

One of the symptoms of depression is a sense of hopelessness, the opposite of confidence. At times my trust has faded so severely I thought of giving up altogether. Yet my belief in God does not die, even when God feels distant. In my heart, I cry out, but I don't feel I'm reaching God. I struggle to find the patience I need. *"Wait for the Lord; be strong and take heart and wait for the Lord."* (Psalm 27:14)

And yet, there are times when I struggle emotionally and the reverse happens. God's Word becomes more powerful than it could possibly be during stable times. Bible verses help me find great peace and hope. At such times, I read *"Come to me, all you who are weary and burdened, and I will give you rest,"* (Matthew 11:28) and my entire being finds relief. I feel comforted. I know these words come from a loving God. These deep spiritual experiences sustain me during rough times; they provide memories I can go back to.

I will never forget the day my friend Helen came to me at a time I felt I couldn't go on. She impressed on me how much I had to live for. She told me she loved me. Whenever I need to remember how great God's love is, I think back to that occasion. Speaking to me through this caring friend, God became powerfully real to me. When I am waiting for depression to lift, I focus on how great God's love has proven to be, time after time.

I feel a kinship with King David who, in Psalm 40, wrote: *"I waited patiently for the Lord; he turned to me and heard my cry."* Waiting patiently is the only thing I can do as I recover from extreme moods. Remembering that God loves me. Trusting.

# Recovery

*"He forgives all my sins and heals all my diseases. He ransoms me from death and surrounds me with love and tender mercies. He fills my life with good things. My youth is renewed like the eagle's." (Psalm 103:3–5)*

WHEN I AM recovering from a bout of depression, I have to resist the temptation to rush back into doing the million things I did before I became sick. Smaller bites become necessary. By breaking up a big job into little ones, I can avoid trying to do everything at once. Stress was one of the reasons I fell. I will have to try, hard as it is, to alter my work- and play-loads. This is an opportune time to make life changes, to reduce my chances of falling into the same trap again.

As I recover, I gradually adjust to the idea that I'm capable of handling my responsibilities on my own again. Slowly but surely, I realize I'm not as much in need of others' help. At first I miss the attention I was getting from supportive friends—I no longer receive the daily phone calls. Normal life needs to return slowly, one day at a time. Gradually, I come to enjoy the process. With time, I feel a big sense of gratitude for my new strength.

Each time I come back from an unstable period, I feel like a new person. Each episode gives me a new appreciation for life. I'm a better person for what I've been through. I can relate to the story Philip Yancey tells in his book, *Soul Survivor: How my Faith Survived the Church.*

Yancey paints a picture of John Donne's struggles to accept the suffering he had undergone. Donne wrote his journal, *Devotions*, while he was close to death for six weeks during London's Great Plague, an epidemic in which one third of Londoners died.

In Yancey's words, Donne came to the following conclusions: "It now seemed clear, though, that those times of affliction, the circumstances he most resented at the time turned out to be the very occasions of spiritual growth...A definite pattern emerged: pain could be transformed, even redeemed, and apparent evil sometimes results in actual good...Suffering not removed may serve as God's tool."[3]

This is true in my own life. My many struggles with mood swings have made me strong and have given me tools with which to serve God by helping others.

# A New Day

*"But one thing I do: Forgetting what is behind and straining toward what is ahead, I press on toward the goal to win the prize for which God has called me heavenward in Christ Jesus." (Philippians 3:13–14)*

EACH NEW DAY brings an opportunity to pick myself up and move ahead. It's a fresh start, a clean slate. The past is history.

Nothing that happened yesterday is so bad I can't leave it behind and, at least for today, look to what is ahead. I don't want to look way out into the distant future. The next few hours are all that matter now.

What will I do today? How will I live today? What will make me happy today? What can I give? Who can I touch base with?

Each day is a precious gift. If I've been feeling down, what can I do today that will help me feel better? Could I ask my favorite friend to go for a walk with me? Could I go out for a special lunch with my husband? Perhaps I could buy some cotton yarn and knit a dish cloth.

Maybe this is the day I could clean up that mess in the kitchen, with some music to make the work easier, even enjoyable. I could make those easy fudge brownies Wes likes so much. That would make him happy.

This is a new day in which I can put one foot in front of the other, gradually walking to a place of greater clarity. Every day I wake up to new possibilities. I wash my face, comb my hair, step into my jeans, pull on my favorite sweatshirt. *"This is the day the Lord has made."*

# Dizzy

WHEN I'M HYPOMANIC, in a mildly manic state, I race from one activity to another, and I begin to feel dizzy. My mind reels with all the things I feel a need to do. It's difficult to stop the feverish pace. I fear I'm going to lose control. After all, it has happened before, many times.

Gradually I realize I must stop. I need to rest, do something quiet, put my feet up. When I take a little time, even twenty minutes, I'm able to refocus on the work I most need to do. I can slow down. Relaxation comes more easily. I take out a piece of paper and make a list of what I have to do. Then I focus on the list, one item at a time, doing my best to shut everything else out of my mind.

Rising to a high is dangerous in many ways. Even the aftermath of a low-grade high is almost certain depression, sometimes short-lived, but often lasting for a long period. To avoid this, I must do all I can to ensure a soft landing. This will be my job for the next while.

I try to stay away from everything that elevates my mood, such as events where there are a lot of people. The mall, camera club meetings and even church tend to increase my high once it has taken hold. Too much physical activity can even be harmful at times like this; working out in the gym may not be a good idea. Upbeat music and the company of other women are too stimulating. I don't shut myself off completely from my friends, but have quiet one-on-one visits with the closest ones over coffee or on the telephone. I tell them what is happening and ask for their help and prayers during this unstable period.

Although I'm tempted to run with the mood, to work on the exciting stuff I enjoy so much, I have to simplify my life as much as possible, postponing all non-essential projects. I putter at the mundane work I enjoy, as well as the chores I don't normally enjoy. I focus on tidying up the clutter in the living room and doing the laundry—all the jobs that have gotten behind.

# Music, an Anchor

MY HEAD SPINS as I'm tempted, at every turn, to run from one part of the house to another, doing the many things I want to do.

Music can often anchor my body and mind. Playing the songs and melodies of Enya, Roger Whittaker and Chopin help keep me in one place—I don't want to miss any of it. In the kitchen, I play a tape on our little tape player while I do the dishes. In the laundry room, ironing the tall stack of clothes I've collected for months even becomes enjoyable when I play music. I put on a record in the family room when I know I need to settle down in my leather chair for a while.

Music is a friend that keeps me company, giving voice to whatever emotions I'm experiencing. Sometimes it speaks so clearly, with such intensity, it's as though I enter the heart of the musician. Listening to my current favorite, Grieg's *Peer Gynt Suite*, I revel in the variety of emotions it expresses. Some parts are powerful and exciting, while others soothe my busy mind. I stay put, close my eyes to listen and come to rest.

# Fear of Symptoms

WHEN I BECOME disorganized, slightly paranoid, or when I feel depression descending, it's easy to become afraid. When I know my mind is over-active and I forget where I parked my car in a busy parking lot, I sometimes verge on panic. With a history of psychosis, it's easy for me to worry I'm going out of control once again. I begin to think to myself: "I'm losing it! I'm going crazy! It's happening again! I'm a hopeless case! Am I going to end up on the psych ward again?"

But I've learned over the years that becoming overly anxious about such things increases my stress level tenfold. I remind myself over and over that losing a car can happen to anyone. "Relax, trust," I tell myself. I take a deep breath, think calmly and retrace my steps, while encouraging myself to believe I will find my car. A sense of control returns.

# One Thing at a Time

IS IT THE maturity of growing older that has helped me learn how to think of only one thing at a time, something I couldn't do when I was younger? I don't know, but it's proving useful. I no longer worry about many problems all at one time. Even when I'm faced with a number of concerns, I can accomplish much when I keep my focus narrow. One small bite at a time, savoring each one individually, helps me cope with my relatively complicated life. *"So don't worry about tomorrow, for tomorrow will bring its own worries. Today's trouble is enough for today."* (Matthew 6:34)

When I do laundry, I center my attention on the work. I separate the whites from the colors; I remove the stains. Nothing else matters at this moment.

When I'm with a friend, I focus on her, paying attention to what we're discussing. I shut out everything else and feel connected.

In church, I sing the songs, pray the prayers and listen to the sermon. Other concerns can wait. They are safely on my to-do list at home, ready for me to deal with at a later time.

When I need to slow down, I use this same narrow focus to engage in the simple and enjoyable pastimes that help me relax. I read a magazine or play a familiar game with Wes. If I can, I take a short nap.

# Clearing the Clutter

BEING OVERWHELMED and disorganized are big problems when my mood is elevated. Forcing myself to slow down is the best way to deal with such times. I focus on cleaning up my surroundings.

Wes and I are hopelessly untidy individuals, never patient enough to stop and put things where they belong. Half the rooms in our house are such disasters that guests are not allowed there. I would be ashamed to have them see them! These parts of the house require much time and patience to organize, not easy to do when I'm feeling high. But the areas where we spend most of our time and entertain visitors are easier to bring under control. Tidying these becomes an excellent project because it is manageable.

I turn on the radio to my favorite station and begin to clean up the living room. Taking my time, I put things where they belong, slowly dealing with one item at a time. I move to the kitchen, wash the dishes in the sink and wipe the table and countertops. I'm surprised at how little time this actually takes, how different the rooms look afterwards, and what a relief I feel when it's done! Sometimes I go a step further and file the stack of recipes I've collected.

All this is good therapy. As I clear the clutter in my home, I clear the clutter in my mind as well. My anxiety is relieved, I no longer feel so overwhelmed—I regain a sense of control.

# Finding Comfort in Scripture

WHEN MY MOOD is high and my mind is too busy, when I'm anxious and can't relax enough to sleep, when I desire peace, I turn to the Bible.

The Bible contains an abundance of wonderful passages to help us deal with almost anything in life. When I'm in trouble, I prefer to focus on one simple, short verse that I can repeat to myself. My memory is poor, so I write it on a little card that I keep close by. One such verse, which has carried me through some of my most difficult times in recent years, is Zephaniah 3:17. *"The Lord your God is with you...he will quiet you with his love."* When I read those words, it is as though God has put his arms around me. God quiets me. I can close my eyes and rest.

# In Spite of the Suffering...

*"...we rejoice in our sufferings, because we know that suffering produces perseverance; perseverance, character; and character, hope." (Romans 5:3–4)*

DISORGANIZATION THAT turned into breaks from reality has led to long periods in hospital for me. Now, when I begin to feel disorganized, I worry. But, as I grow older and more mature in my faith, I have learned not to panic. When I leave an empty frying pan cooking on the stove, or do some other such forgetful thing, I try not to be concerned. I go easy on myself. I might mutter "stupid me" under my breath, but I make an effort to slow myself down. My faith in God has helped me attain this more positive approach. I don't need to worry; I can trust God to be with me.

Looking at my poor health, physical as well as emotional, from a positive and light-hearted point of view helps me cope. I delight in my good times, and I'm learning to approach the poor times with a sense of hope. In a strange way, most of the depression I've experienced lately—thankfully a mild form—has been tinged with a touch of gladness. When I meet my friends, my misery turns to mild joy. I think it must be love that allows me to feel this joy, the love God has taught me to have for my friends.

I've been lucky. My recent depression was not the kind that leaves me with that sense of hopelessness so much a part of this condition. I am aware of what my disorder can do to me, and I'm sure things will not always be easy for me. Yet I've read of many members of God's family who are able to find joy in the midst of their suffering. Such intervals of joy are possible—maybe for me as well.

Jake Hess, one of the Gaithers group of singers, is a good example of what it means to bring joy into the midst of tough situations. Hess suffered from multiple health problems and came close to death several times before he was felled by a heart attack in 2004. But his desire to sing kept him going. He loved God and desired nothing more than to witness through the songs he wrote and sang. Some of his songs had depressing words, such as the one about his body being "wore out," but he performed them with humor, his face glowing and his eyes twinkling. He made fun of what he suffered. And through it all, he thanked God for being in his life and giving him a song to sing. His spirit was contagious, and his audience loved him for it.

Jake Hess inspires me, and I'm sure many others, to approach my difficulties in the same way.

# Midnight Scribblings

*Almost every night nowadays I awake, as I do at 2 a.m. tonight. I want, and need, to fall asleep again. But experience has taught me I will first need to get a few things off my mind and onto paper. And how neat it is to go through this process!*

*As thoughts tumble out, I write. I'm not sure whether what ends up on the page will be useful for anything, but I write anyway.*

*I pray to God, "Thank you for this time. May my words be sincere and honest."*

*A brief prayer and then, hopefully, more sleep until the time to arise and begin a new day.*

# Journaling

I HAVEN'T BEEN truly manic for many years now, but the milder hypomania comes often. Lately I've experienced this hypomania, along with periods of anxiety and depression. This is what my psychiatrist calls "a mixed state."

Strange and interesting, but worrisome as well: The last time I was in hospital, I was writing *Riding the Roller Coaster*. I wrote about my hospitalization and how I had been depressed for a year and a half. At the time, I was bordering on suicide; at least, I wished I were dead.

I remember sitting on my bed writing. In the dismal hospital setting, writing gave me pleasure. It was something useful to do. I wanted my book to help others who suffered as I did.

Today I wonder: If I wrote my first book at such a difficult time, and now I'm writing my second book at a difficult time, am I doing this because of my severe mood swing? Or is the writing the cause of my mood swing? Is this book you're holding in your hands the cause or the result of the mixed and hypomanic mood I've experienced since I began working on it?

Yet the writing comforts me. It helps me sort out my thoughts and deal with my pain. It is something I must do. What I'm learning about myself right now could benefit others with bipolar disorder. If it can do that, then this struggle will be worthwhile. If I have to suffer, I may as well make it count for something.

I pray to God I won't land in hospital again. I pray I will be able to keep functioning well. If I need to cry, God, let it be at night so that, as David (who knew about such things) wrote, *"weeping may remain for a night, but rejoicing comes in the morning."* (Psalm 30:5b)

# From High to Low

*Yesterday I felt like a busy octopus, pulled in a multitude of directions by all the things I needed to do. I felt as though I had no time to waste and jumped from writing a letter to doing the laundry to calling a friend to working on a photography assignment to cooking a meal to cleaning a room. I felt as though I was racing, and, although I wasn't physically out of breath, my mind felt out of breath. I was emotionally dizzy, yet I could not stop, I could not rest.*

*But this morning was quite different. I awoke with a sense of peace. I relished the comfort of languishing in bed with my third mug of coffee. I was slightly tearful, but even that felt kind of good. Such a relief from the pressured living of yesterday! Yet, with this reprieve came a gradual desire not to do anything at all.*

*I knew I would now have to take care not to let this new restfulness suck me under. This is the danger I face at times like this. A sudden drop from an overly busy state to being overly relaxed can lead to depression. In the past, such depressions have pulled me down for weeks and even months at a time. I cannot let this happen. How I live today is critical. Although I know I cannot always fend off such misery, I know there is much I can do to try.*

# The Gift of Sleep

*"I lie down and sleep; I wake again, because the Lord sustains me." (Psalm 3:5)*

I HAVE SPENT quite a bit of my time over the last year and a half in a mildly hypomanic state. I've been high enough to write endlessly, but not so as to become concerned about lack of sleep. Although I don't need much sleep, I worry occasionally that my mood will be so heightened that lack of rest will become a problem. Insufficient sleep can cause full-blown mania.

Though my head spins with things I want to do, I haven't had trouble taking catnaps. What a gift this trust in God has given me! Trust enables me to let go and rest even when my mind is so very busy. *"He makes me lie down in green pastures...he restores my soul"* (Psalm 23:2)

What a blessing to sleep and awake a few minutes later refreshed! My mind moves at a slower pace; I'm more at peace. Each time I get up from one of these naps, I'm refreshed and renewed, ready again to enjoy the life God has given me, a life full of interesting work to do.

*Chapter 6*

# OVERCOMING THE
# STIGMA

## Misconceptions

I'M DISAPPOINTED WHEN friends and family who know me well say things that reveal a gross misunderstanding of depression and how it affects those of us who suffer from it. One person close to me thought depression was something we bring on when we feel sorry for ourselves. Perhaps she thought we liked the attention.

Sufferers of depression would do anything to feel happy and vibrant again. When I'm depressed, many friends keep me at arm's length. I don't blame them. It's not pleasant to be around me when I can't find anything to talk about except my pain. Depression does that to you: It turns your thinking inward; all you can wrap your mind around is the misery you feel. You end up feeling very alone.

Another person complained to me about an acquaintance with depression who couldn't manage to do anything more than lie on the sofa. "Couldn't he just try and make himself do something?" she asked. Nothing I said could convince her that this was an illness that, like other illnesses, couldn't be helped by simple willpower.

Those who have never experienced depression find it difficult to understand how profoundly a brain disorder can affect the entire body.

A long time ago, when I was bordering on psychosis, my doctor put me in a seniors' care facility for a few days to give me relief from the stress I faced at home. I called a close family member to let her know where I was. She advised me, "You've got to pull yourself together and be strong. You have to try harder." That was insensitive. I was at the facility because I was doing my best to recover—I wasn't living with eighty and ninety-year-olds for fun. She should have known I always try my best. When I'm trapped in this state, extricating myself is extremely hard. I need time and medication to recover. If I sound angry and hurt, yes, I was.

A person I worked with recommended strongly that I get counseling. "You don't need those pills you're taking. All you need is to talk to someone at my church." She knew nothing about mental disorders like mine. She had no idea what I was dealing with. Again, I seethed, remembering how psychotic I was when I was first admitted to hospital. I could become sick like that again if I didn't take the medication my mental stability depended on. Would this person tell a diabetic to stop taking insulin?

Christian psychiatrist and author, Dwight L. Carlson, writes, "There are legions of God-fearing Christians who—to the best of their ability—are walking according to the Scriptures and yet are suffering from emotional symptoms. Many of them have been judged for their condition and given half-truths and clichés by well-meaning but ill-informed fellow believers. 'Pray for God's forgiveness,' some are told. 'A person who is right with the Lord can't have a nervous breakdown.'"[4]

Fortunately, I have not been treated in this way. The church congregations I've belonged to have been understanding, yet the stigma continues. It hurts me deeply that Christians who should be compassionate are often judgmental. Church communities need to learn the medical basis for mental disorders and how that differs from the spiritual. They are in the best position to help those in crisis. But when they don't understand, they are in danger of doing a lot of damage. For Christians, there is nothing worse than to be told our emotional problems are our own fault, the result of unconfessed sin. We suffer so much already. Having to shoulder blame multiplies our mental anguish.

# Stigma

THE FEELING OF shame that comes with a diagnosis of mental illness is the biggest reason the diagnosis is so difficult to accept. The stigma is the most unjust and regrettable aspect of living with these diseases. Many suffer in silence, feeling forced to keep their illness secret. They receive limited support, which adds to their hardship. Stigma comes from ingrained ignorance that has existed for most of recorded history.

Because of stigma, less money has been available for mental health research than for almost any other major disease. The public does not feel empathy for sufferers of mental illness and therefore does not support fundraising campaigns like those for cancer and heart research.

According to the American Psychiatric Association, "Raymond DePaulo, M.D., the Henry Phipps professor and chair of psychiatry and behavioral sciences at Johns Hopkins University, reports that federal research on mental illness, including substance abuse, continues to be underfunded compared with other medical illnesses like diabetes or cancer." DePaulo "...was optimistic that funding will increase for research on depression and other mental illnesses much as it has for cancer. 'Depression and other psychiatric illnesses are misunderstood and underfunded in the way cancer research was in the late 1960s. There was a stigma about cancer, a lot of misinformation, and only a few poorly understood treatments.'"[5]

Much of society still sees mental illness as a sign of weak character, of not being able to cope with life. Many blame [or cast blame on] those with bipolar disorder. Others think, incorrectly, that a person with bipolar disorder is always sick, never "normal." We have all heard the myriad disparaging remarks and names in reference to patients and the hospitals that care for them. No wonder such a strong feeling of guilt and humiliation comes with the illness. No wonder so many of us deny that we have a problem and refuse medical treatment.

Lack of education is mostly to blame for this stigma. If society were better informed, there would be far less reason for shame. If those of us living with mental illness were able to tell others about it and its causes, there would be less need for secrecy. Unfortunately, many do not have that freedom. They need to maintain their ability to earn a living. As long as prejudice exists, revealing their disorder can threaten their livelihood.

In recent years, much has been learned about the causes of bipolar disorder and other brain diseases. As far back as 1991, Lewis L. Judd, former director of the National Institute of Mental Health, reported that 90% of all that is known about the human brain was discovered in the past ten years.[6] Effective medication for mental illnesses has only been around for the past few decades, allowing many who would in the past have spent their lives in mental hospitals to lead productive lives.

Researchers are proving the biochemical nature of the most common mental illnesses. Yet so much of society still clings to old ideas, unaware of medical truths. In this age of understanding, the time has come for better awareness of the organic causes of mental illness. In the western world, where most children receive a high school education, knowledge of such things should be widespread. I sincerely hope that, one day, those living with mental illness will be able to speak freely about it while receiving the respect and support they need and deserve.

# Why Nobody Talks About It

MENTAL ILLNESS IS common. According to the National Alliance on Mental Illness (NAMI), twenty to twenty-five percent of individuals will be affected by some form of mental illness during their lifetime. There are few people without a family member or friend who suffers from some form of mental illness. Mental illness is more common than cancer, diabetes, heart disease or AIDS. Why, then, does nobody talk about it?

Isabella Mori, a psychotherapist living in Vancouver, describes the problem very well:

> "Most of us know very little about mental illness, and ignorance breeds fear. Fear breeds avoidance. Avoidance breeds more ignorance. It's a vicious cycle. And vicious cycles breed more vicious cycles: The ignorance that prevents us from learning more about mental illness does not only create more fear and avoidance in us, but also prevents people who have a mental illness from talking about it. This makes them more afraid, and therefore more prone to isolate from people who they feel don't understand them—and that exacerbates the symptoms of mental illness."[7]

If we are to eradicate the stigma, we need to educate people. We have to find a way to break the cycle of ignorance, fear and avoidance. At one time, cancer was a stigmatized disease as well. But, thanks to education, people don't fear it quite so much.

When a person has cancer, she can talk about it without shame. Funds have been raised for research; more effective treatments have been discovered. I believe the same will one day be possible for mental illnesses.

# Stories from the Funny Farm

THE CRUELTY OF the stigma toward mental illness disturbs me greatly. When I was in high school, years before I had any idea I would one day become a victim of mental illness, a teacher told us about her "time at Essondale," another name for the major psychiatric facility, Riverview Hospital. Before she could say more, the class burst out laughing. Ignoring the snickering, she carried on telling us about the work she had done there.

The students' reaction was not the only thing wrong here. It seemed to me that the teacher herself was aware of the response her first words would bring. Would it not have been better to talk about "her time *working* at Essondale?" Having later spent months at that institution as a patient, I now look back on that incident and realize they were laughing about me.

Some years later, during a conversation with friends, one of them mentioned the people at the "funny farm." She had no idea I had spent nine months there. She had no idea how it hurt to hear such an offhand reference to unfortunate people. I didn't say anything, but I will never forget the comment. My opinion of her plummeted. She was not the kind of friend I could ever confide in.

The many individuals who harbor such prejudice don't consider that they are talking about real people, people not unlike themselves, people who are suffering. Those who haven't experienced mental illness, or been close to someone who has, have no idea what a mental disorder can mean. They don't realize they could very well be a victim one day. No one is immune.

A big innovation—deinstitutionalizing the mentally ill—has caused a major reduction in treatment in many parts of North America. Mental hospitals like the one I spent time in are depressing places with impersonal, inadequate care, and the closing of beds may have been good in a way. Yet, alternate care has, in many cases, not been provided. Countless individuals have ended up on the streets. Instead of taking medication to manage their illness, they consume alcohol and street drugs to help them cope, leading to addiction. If such negligence were shown toward those suffering from physical medical conditions, the public would be outraged.

Nevertheless, in spite of this tragic reduction in hospital beds, society seems to be developing a more mature attitude toward people with psychiatric disorders. The mental health organizations which have sprung up are devoted to educating the public and advocating for us. Support groups are easier to find. The improved understanding of brain disorders encourages many of us to come forward to tell our stories and inform others. I haven't heard stories about the "funny farm" for quite some time. I hope I'm not being overly optimistic when I say that the world is becoming a friendlier, more compassionate place for us.

## Accepting Myself

UNFORTUNATELY, MUCH stigma is rooted within our own minds, within the minds of those who suffer from the disorders. We grew up hearing stories about "the loonie, the nut case, the weirdo, the schizo, the person who is not all there." These views have been around for so long, they're difficult to shake. When we are diagnosed with bipolar disorder, we're shocked, afraid and ashamed to find out we, ourselves, are now among this group of the rejected, the scorned, the ridiculed and, yes, the feared.

Yet I have come to see my disorder for what it is: a disease that affects the brain, an organ of the body. It has nothing to do with my personality. I view myself as the complete, worthy individual I am. There is no need for shame. If I can walk confidently down my path in life, with a good image of myself, if I trust that I can overcome my difficulties, then I can overcome the stigma. I'm comfortable in the knowledge that I am one of God's children. God has a plan for my life, as he has plans for others' lives.

In the days he walked the earth, Jesus expressed love for everyone. But he especially showed compassion toward those who were most looked down on and shunned: those with the much-feared epilepsy; the hated tax collectors; the shameful prostitutes; those believed to harbor evil spirits. Jesus touched the lives of these people in a most personal way—he treated them as worthy individuals. Their lives were changed immeasurably.

Reading how Christ loved the stigmatized helps me, more than ever, appreciate how he loves me. I realize how wrong stigma is. The story of Jesus encourages me to work at building a better understanding, especially in the fellowship of believers.

## Accepting the Tough Facts

MANY PEOPLE WHO struggle with mood disorders are in denial. Only one out of three living with depression or manic depression will look for help. Only one out of ten will seek treatment from a medical doctor trained to treat such illnesses.[8]

The diagnosis of bipolar disorder is tough to accept. No one would want or, at first, even believe such a diagnosis. Anyone would be inclined to think, "This is something other people have—certainly not me." Because of the stigma attached to mental illness, most of us would rather be diagnosed with a physical illness, even a serious one. None of us likes to think of ourselves as "not right in the head."

"Maybe it's only a phase I have to work through," we might think, and then try to overcome the difficulties on our own, often without success. When things don't get better, we begin to feel guilt and shame. Sometimes we believe the problem is spiritual.

In a manic state, we might find it especially hard to believe anything could be wrong, though it is obvious to those close to us. We feel better than ever: happy, energetic, confident and focused. We might become creative and wrapped up in any number of grandiose schemes that make sense to us but leave family and friends concerned. They see that we're "out of control, an embarrassment," but they can't convince us something is wrong and we need medical help. A person in the midst of mania believes this is the super-achiever she was meant to be and this euphoria will never leave her.

Bipolar disorder most often strikes in early adulthood, a time when the diagnosis is somewhat easier to cope with. Those struck later in life find the diagnosis more difficult to accept. A person who has always thought of himself as a competent individual, with years invested in a career and reputation, will be particularly hard hit. Relationships often cannot withstand the strain, and marriages break up.

Few of us would hesitate to take a pain killer for a headache or an antibiotic for an infection. Yet we would deny being sick and refuse treatment rather than take a psychiatric drug. Something about taking medication to make our brain work more normally instills fear and shame—it says we are abnormal or different. We are afraid our mind will be harmed or be made to work unnaturally. We worry about side effects. Tragically, far too many sufferers deny themselves the relief today's medical treatment can bring. They miss the opportunity for a more normal life.

# I Find Out I'm Not Alone

FOR TEN YEARS after I was in the psychiatric hospital, Crease Clinic, I had no idea what was wrong with me. My doctor had never given me a diagnosis, and I hadn't asked for one. Naively, I assumed whatever was wrong was unique to me. I did not think there was a name for it. I felt special, though of course not in a good way. It never occurred to me to find out more.

One day I read a newspaper story about a violent murder carried out by a man with a mental disorder called manic depression. I had heard of this illness and knew it was serious. I read the description in the article and, to my amazement, discovered that the symptoms matched mine. This was the first time I realized my disorder was a common but frightening condition. The only difference between this man and me seemed to be that I had no tendency toward violence, even in a psychotic state. (For a small number of people, violence and anger come with the disorder.)

116

Since first becoming sick, I have never denied I had a mental health condition. The reality was thrust on me when I had a total breakdown and spent nine months in a psychiatric facility. Yet I took awhile longer to learn to live with the idea of an illness with the terrible label "manic depression." In time, I came to appreciate having a disorder that actually had a name. I learned there were others who experienced life as I did, and I came to better understand what I occasionally went through. I found out I wasn't alone. There were even support groups for people like me.

Much later I learned a clear diagnosis had been difficult in the early years of my illness. Symptoms I displayed suggested either schizophrenia or manic depression. My current doctor is now certain I have manic depression. The diagnosis no longer upsets me. Knowing what to call it has helped me research and understand it better. I appreciate the new medication that has come available. The world of medicine has come a long way, and manic depression is no longer as scary a diagnosis as it once was. Even its new name, "bipolar disorder," makes it more comfortable to live with. Coping with the illness today is much easier than it was twenty years ago.

## Coming Out

I HAVE NEVER been good at keeping secrets. A few months after I was released from Riverview, I went to the manager of the office where I had worked one summer. Rather than keep my illness quiet, I was honest about what had happened to me. I told him I had spent time in a mental hospital. "But," I said, "I have to work if I'm going to be well. Would you let me work for nothing until I have rehabilitated myself and become useful to you again?" To my delight, he took me on. I'll be forever indebted to this man for the chance he gave me. Once I got better, he entrusted me with interesting, challenging work I took pride in, work that built my self-esteem at a time when I needed it badly. And, though I would have been happy to work for free, I was paid a few dollars, even for those first few weeks when I did not accomplish much.

I don't usually talk about my background until I know a person well enough to trust her—and only then if there is good reason to do so. I would much rather describe my condition myself than have it whispered about behind my back. My disorder will always be with me, and I need friends who can understand what's happening when I have an episode. How else will they learn the true nature of my illness and not simply think of me as "weird"? How else can I ensure I will have support when I need it?

I explain my problems casually, without suggesting I feel ashamed—because I truly don't. When people with mental illness internalize the stigma, feeling embarrassed and being secretive about their history, they encourage others to continue the unfortunate cycle of stigma.

When the damaging effect of this stigma was weighing heavy on my mind, I met with Bev Gutray, the executive director of the B.C. Division of the Canadian Mental Health Association (CMHA). She treated me with more respect than I had imagined possible from a professional who knew I had a bipolar disorder. Bev took the time to photocopy reams of reports and information that would help me understand the problems stigma was causing. I went home with a bulging briefcase. Thus began my volunteer work with this organization.

My anger over the stigma I witnessed fueled my decision to make my life with the disorder public. At the CMHA, I became involved in interesting projects in the publishing department, and I learned to speak and write freely about my disorder without the least shame. In spite of the abundance of knowledge that had become available, my anger persisted. I saw stigma as the major culprit keeping people with mental illness from accepting their condition and obtaining treatment.

A quote by Dr. John Varsamis, M.D., originally published in the April 1990 newsletter of the Society for Depression and Manic

Depression of Manitoba, impacted my determination to become active. Dr. Varsamis wrote: "Mental illness is so common that if even a small proportion of the patients made a special effort to learn as much as they could about their illness and if they proceeded to educate their families and friends, there would not be too many uninformed people left and the stigma associated with mental illness would be virtually eradicated." If I wanted something done about this, it would have to start with me.

In 1993 I wrote an article entitled *Sick, But No One Brought Me Flowers*, a description of what it was like to be sick and in a mental hospital. I submitted it to our major daily newspaper, the *Vancouver Sun*, for their popular *Voices* column, which featured personal stories from readers. To my surprise, the paper agreed to publish it. The piece appeared on the third page, prominent and with my photograph. All of a sudden, every corner of my world knew my history: members of my camera club, fellow churchgoers, neighbors, my son's friends and their parents.

That first article took courage to publish, but I have never regretted it. None of the subsequent speaking engagements or writing required courage (though public speaking still makes me a little nervous). As I said to a friend, "Once I dived in, I found the water was fine."

In the following years, I wrote more articles for newspapers and magazines, and I published my first book, *Riding the Roller Coaster*. My purpose was, and continues to be, to build awareness and help those who also have my disorder. I want to lessen the fear individuals experience when they first receive their diagnosis. I want to inform the public so that they will have a better understanding and be more willing to accept us as equal members of the community.

There may be people who think I'm odd because of my illness, and I've lost one or two friends through my openness about it. Some people don't think such things should be discussed. Losing friends is painful, but I've had to take this stand. I feel good about who I am, and I know I'm right to speak out. What's more, I'm finding most friends and acquaintances accept and support me and what I do—they respect me for it.

My decision to speak out came less than four years after I accepted Christ as my savior. Sometimes I wonder: Would I have had the courage to go public if I didn't know God was with me and loved me? How much did my trust in God help me take that initial plunge to publish the newspaper story?

Jesus helped me finally realize I was created for a purpose—he made an overwhelming change in my life. The apostle Paul said, *"It's in Christ that we find out who we are and what we are living for."* (Ephesians 1:11, MSG) I feel strongly that God has created me to do this work. Though it can be frustrating at times, it gives me fulfillment and joy.

Stigma towards the mentally ill will take a long time to eradicate. I doubt it will happen in my lifetime. Every little bit we do to educate people will help reduce it. Those of us who have the courage to speak out must continue to do so.

*Chapter 7*

# LIVING
# DAY BY DAY

## Beginning the Day

I LOVE GETTING up in the morning. Amazing what a difference a night's rest can make. I feel better and have a better outlook! As I awake around 6:00 or 6:30 a.m., my heart fills with anticipation for the hour or two that lie ahead. Before I swing my legs out of bed, I say a few words of thanks to God.

This precious time is my favorite part of the day. I put on my slippers and bathrobe, slip my watch around my wrist and raise the thermostat in the hallway. Downstairs I grab a cup of coffee and seat myself comfortably in my favorite chair, a big leather one with a roomy hammock for my feet.

My meditation time involves a number of activities. I have no set agenda but let my mind go wherever the Spirit moves me. As I sip my coffee, I pray, read my Bible, write or listen to some of my favorite music. Sometimes I just sit and mull things over in my mind. I doze off now and then. My plans for the day don't enter my mind until I have drunk fully, nourished by what God gives me.

The only distraction is my cat, Max, who has also come to love these morning times. He eagerly jumps onto my lap and kneads his sharp claws into the arm of my terry bathrobe. It hurts a little, but I hate to push him away. Eventually he settles down and curls up on my knees for the last portion of his night's sleep. He makes it difficult when I want to rest my Bible on my lap, get up for another cup of coffee or put on another record. But I'm reluctant to make him move when he's so comfortable.

When my stomach asks for breakfast, I know it's time to gear up for what I want to bring to the rest of the day. I look at my planner and prepare to work on the first item.

# Getting Organized

NOT HAVING A job outside the home means my life is unstructured. It would be so easy to waste away the hours of the day, uncertain of what I should do. Things in my head can disappear in the tangle of my busy life. They roam about my mind, leaving me thinking about them endlessly. I become worn out and stressed before I even begin the work. The answer for me has been to make lists, lists that will keep me on track and help me sort out what needs to be done.

I make to-do lists, shopping lists, lists of menus. Before I go to bed each night, I write in my planner the things I'd like to accomplish the next day, leaving plenty of margin for the last minute distractions that always come along. Waking up with a ready-made plan helps me get the day moving. Every day has a purpose.

Dumping everything from my mind onto paper helps me survive. It frees me from the clutter of worries I might otherwise have. Organizing lists helps especially when I feel overwhelmed or depressed. At such times I keep them to a few manageable items. I try not to crowd too many "must-do's" into a single day unless I'm truly healthy.

Having lost much time to illness, I've come to value my good health. Each day of wellness is precious, each moment is precious. I try to make the most of them. My to-do list includes all the projects and jobs I need to do, from dishes or laundry to writing a magazine article. It also includes those things I do simply because I enjoy them, such as preparing a photography display for my doctor's waiting room or making note cards. A large project sometimes requires a list of its own, broken up into manageable portions. When I was doing publicity work for a weekend retreat, for example, I made a separate list for this, itemizing what I needed to do.

I feel in control when I can decide on which item to tackle first. When it's done, I can cross it out and clear it from my mind. The most important jobs come first. But I also like to give some priority to easier chores. When I can do something quickly, I'm able to cross it off and reduce the length of the list faster.

Often my moods will dictate which items I should work on. I would have to be in a very good mood to be able to clean up my workshop, a disaster area. And sometimes I'm too disorganized to manage paying the bills. Then, weeding the garden might be a better project. Sometimes my energy is low, and the best thing is to visit with a friend to have coffee or watch a video. Being flexible helps me get the most out of my days.

Without having these lists to show me clearly what needs to be done, I would not be able to function effectively. My life would be far different from what it is today. My days and weeks are rich, in large part because my lists encourage me to carry out a wide assortment of activities.

# Finding Balance in Variety

*"There is a time for everything, and a season for every activity under heaven:" (Ecclesiastes 3:1)*

EVERY DAY CAN be a day to look forward to if I have well-balanced plans. I feel pleased when I look ahead and see a day that includes some giving and some receiving; some work and some play; some busyness and some restfulness. I get work done and have some fun as well. Even the housecleaning is enjoyable if I know it will be rewarded by a visit from friends. Good plans pay off, making my life rich yet free of stress. This is the ideal, but it doesn't always happen. And then I'm in trouble!

Far too often, I become passionately involved in something important to me, such as raising awareness about mental health issues. I forget to relax, and I wake up to the morning consumed by thoughts of the many things I need to do: difficult and stressful writing and phone calls. My mind becomes preoccupied with the world's problems and the plans I need to make to help solve them. I feel frustrated, I feel angry. I forget about having fun, I forget about resting.

I have to remember to balance my lifestyle if I'm to stay healthy. I belong to a variety of communities: a photography club, a writers' group, a church, a Bible study group, and church and online mood-disorder support groups. My participation in all of these encourages me to be creative, visually and verbally. They also feed my spiritual needs. I have responsibilities to some of these groups, responsibilities I enjoy. This helps me play a part in my communities' welfare. Contributing to these groups is important to me. Problems often arise, though, when I become overwhelmed by the tasks I take on. Then I need to step back and decide what I should carry on doing and what I should drop. I hate doing that!

Relationships are also important to me. I need to feel socially connected with my friends and family. Each day, I try to spend time with someone, whether it's through a visit or phone call, whether we play or work together. Wes and I try to work in a game of cribbage whenever we can. It unwinds us both and provides us with some of the time together we need.

My daily lists help build this balance into my life.

# Alternating Work and Play

MANY YEARS AGO, I passed through a long period of depression that lasted over a year. My son was in elementary school, and most of my responsibilities were toward him and my household. Apart from that, nothing exciting was happening in my life. I was bored. Motivating myself to do chores was a great problem, but I found a solution, something that encouraged me to keep up with my chores.

I've always loved to knit, crochet and do cross-stitching and needlepoint projects. There's nothing like creative work to color a dismal day. During this difficult period of my life, I decided to knit a sweater. Knitting is a relaxing pastime. I can sit in my most comfortable chair and listen to music or watch television while I work. No need to feel guilty about being lazy. I am, after all, being productive.

But I could have stayed in that chair and worked on my knitting all day. That would definitely have made me feel guilty, and justly so. I decided to play a game with myself. If I could do one hour of housework, I would reward myself with an hour of knitting.

This plan worked well. I was able to finish my chores, never feeling too bogged down by them. This program provided days I could look forward to, even if my mood was down. Every hour counted for something. Getting up in the morning was not as difficult as it might have been.

# Taking Care of the Whole Me

THE OLDER I GET, the more I realize that my emotional wellness depends to a large extent on how well I take care of the whole me: my body, mind and spirit. All parts of me have a bearing on how well I am able to live and how healthy I will be. Each part helps the others to function. All are interconnected.

I've learned, somewhat late in life, to take care of my body by maintaining a good diet, exercising and resting. This is necessary, not only for my body's sake, but also for the good of my mind and soul. *Every* part of us belongs to God. As Paul said in 1 Corinthians 6:19 & 20, *"...your body is a temple of the Holy Spirit, who is in you, whom you have received from God...You are not your own; you were bought at a price. Therefore honor God with your body."* How could I possibly do the work God has led me to do without a healthy body and mind?

I feed my mind by reading and learning. I receive stimulation from socializing with friends and engaging in creative activities. These in turn feed me spiritually by giving me a sense of fulfillment and joy. They provide me with feelings of gratitude and well-being.

I further feed myself spiritually by starting each day with prayer and Bible reading. These times help me feel closer to God; they help me understand the direction I need to take. God encourages me to move forward in the work I set out for each day. God helps me build the positive attitude that makes me want to stay healthy. I'm inspired to look after my mind and my body.

As with many other illnesses, the attitude I bring to my treatment has a large bearing on how quickly I recover from an episode. I must emphasize again, medication is important. I can't function very long without it. Yet simply taking pills and making no other effort is not enough. To receive a prescription from the doctor and then sit in front of the television, waiting for the medication to work, won't do. I have to apply a healthy lifestyle to my recovery plan. My whole self has to be involved in the healing process. I must feed my body, mind and spirit. Often I feed myself by feeding others. By giving to others I receive back.

We've all heard stories of inspiration. They tell us how individuals with severe struggles—situational, physical, emotional and spiritual—manage to overcome them and do well. A positive attitude, healthy living and strong faith did wonders for these people's lives. I believe the same is possible for those who live with mental illness.

## The Importance of a Well-Ordered Life

REGULAR ROUTINE IS healthy. Consistent habits help me to eat well, take my medication, brush my teeth. I'm fortunate to have a husband who encourages good routine. Wes likes to have meals at regular times each day. Lunch is always at noon; supper is always between 5:00 and 6:00 p.m. We never skip a meal, though sometimes we might get lazy and make something simple like soup and a bun for dinner. Sharing our lives helps us stay on schedule because we have established customary habits.

Difficulties come up, though, when Wes goes out of town and I'm not bound to our usual routine. If my mood is not stable, I often forget to eat or go to bed at a decent time. Sometimes I even miss taking my medication. When I'm immersed in reading a book or writing an article, or even just sitting in thought, I have no one to remind me of the time. All discipline goes. My life becomes an unstructured mess. I go hungry, though I don't notice it, and I sleep too much or too little. My mood, not good to begin with, deteriorates even further.

A friend told me about a difficult period of depression in her life. Because she lived on her own, she had no one to remind her of the time. She had no one near who could help her keep a perspective on where she was or should be in relation to the world. She became as if encased in a cocoon. She forgot to give herself the basic needs her body required. She did not exercise, sleep, eat or drink. Her problems became magnified when she forgot to take her medication. If she had only had a friend to touch base with each day, she would not have deteriorated as much as she did.

## The Gifts of Hunger, Thirst and Fatigue

PHILIP YANCEY QUOTES Dr. Paul Brand, a foremost expert on leprosy: "Thank God for inventing pain!" Yancey goes on to say, "He knew that people with diseases like leprosy and diabetes were in grave danger of losing fingers, toes and even entire limbs simply because their warning system of pain had been silenced. They were literally destroying themselves unawares."[9]

In the same way, I should thank God when I sense the need to eat, drink and rest. During extreme moods, either these disappear or I become too busy to pay attention. When I'm in the midst of a high, and especially when Wes is out of town, I'm in that danger. I don't respond to my body's needs. It's so easy to lose track of time when I'm preoccupied with my inner life. I forget everything else.

When my mood is unstable, I'm relieved when my body tells me I'm hungry or need to take a nap. Then I know all is well, and I'm not too badly off. When I have that nagging sensation of needing a snack, I'm happy. It's good and proper to be reminded of my body's needs. I then have an opportunity to eat something that will nourish my body. Not sensing this hunger is an indication that my mental or physical health is suffering.

So, when hunger comes, I try not to put off responding. If it's mealtime, I make some time to prepare a tasty, colorful meal. If it isn't yet time for a full meal, I snack, grabbing an apple, some almonds or yogurt. I try to focus on the taste, appreciating what God has provided.

## Dealing with Sleeplessness

LONG PERIODS OF sleeplessness can be a symptom of both depression and mania. Everyone with bipolar disorder struggles with this problem off and on. During hypomania, a person is able to function for long periods on only four or five hours a night. He may not complain about it, truly feeling that he's getting all the rest he requires. Yet, over a period of time, this can trigger full-blown mania or a psychotic episode.

But occasional bouts of sleeplessness need not be regarded with impatience. I have a friend who often wakes in the middle of the night. She does not look at this with annoyance. In her words, "I think to myself, God must have someone he wants me to pray for." Then she spends the next while in prayer for the many people she cares for. Before she knows it, she is asleep again. She awakes hours later refreshed. "The problem is," she says, "I must change the order of my prayer list once in a while. I tend to fall asleep too fast and only get through the first part of my list. Some of my friends aren't getting as much prayer as they should."

At a time when my doctor changed my medication, my sleep became seriously disturbed. It was the first time in my adult life I was put on a non-sedative antipsychotic. I awoke at all hours of the night—wide awake—and stayed that way for long periods. This went on for several weeks while my body adjusted to the new pills. I very much wanted to give this new treatment a chance to work and decided to accept this side effect with a positive spirit.

These sleepless nights became my opportunity to do some serious reading, something I did not have much time for during daylight hours. They enabled me to read one of the best and longest novels ever written, Dostoevsky's *Brothers Karamazov*. My sleepless nights became a time of enrichment. I read a book I would never have read if I hadn't been going through such problems.

Fortunately God has blessed me with the ability to lie down for brief twenty-minute catnaps, after which I awake refreshed. During that time, I caught up on my rest by taking these frequent naps. This experience taught me not to become too upset when I can't sleep. I've come to think of times of sleeplessness as God-given, as much as my sleeping times are.

I know it does no good to worry if I can't sleep. Everything God gives me can be used for a purpose. Every minute of my days and nights can count for something. Even wakeful times, times when I would rather be sleeping, can be valuable if I look at them that way. I only need to worry when sleeplessness becomes a pattern. Then it is time to check with the doctor.

# A Living Sacrifice

*"Therefore, I urge you, brothers, in view of God's mercy, to offer your bodies as living sacrifices, holy and pleasing to God—this is your spiritual act of worship."* (Romans 12:1)

A COUPLE OF years ago when I began my child photography business, I decided I must do something to get fit and stay fit. Making candid photographs of young children means being able to crouch at their level as they play. I need to crawl and wriggle my body around on the floor to find the best position to capture the shots I want. As I work, I am up and down, constantly bending my knees, constantly lowering my body and bringing it back up. At my age, the level of fitness this requires is not automatic. I was going to have to work at it.

For the first time in my life, I took out membership at a gym. I learned the joys of moving my body vigorously. I learned what it means to expend energy and then to gain back more than I had before. I came to love going and feel badly when I couldn't.

I enjoy the social aspects of the workouts as well. At my all-women's club, the machines are positioned in a circle, facing each other. We change stations every thirty seconds, so I am never bored. As we move around the room, we socialize. There are opportunities, however brief, to share some of the good and some of the bad that might be preoccupying our minds. Not only does my body benefit from the workout, my mood does as well. This is a good way to begin the day.

I have come to understand how important it is to respect and take care of the body God has given me. Having a healthy body allows me to fulfill what I want to do with my life. By ensuring I eat well and exercise and rest sufficiently, I am doing my best to be all I can be for God. I want to fulfill the purposes God has for me—I have to do my part to make that possible.

# Smiles

WHEN MY MOOD is good and I have the opportunity to begin the day with a quiet time of devotion, it is not hard to go out the door with a smile on my face. I don't even have to make an effort. When I look them in the eye and smile, store clerks become friendlier, people I pass on the street smile back. I become approachable; I become someone they would like to talk to.

Some time ago, when my mood was not good, I was not able to bring that smile to my face. As I worked out at the gym, I struggled to feel a part of what was happening around me. My body was sluggish. The other women in the gym seemed rather glum as well.

But suddenly everything changed. Someone walked in with a big grin on her face and laughter in her voice. The room soon exploded, filled with fun. It's amazing how that one person brought our feelings up and made us smile. My day immediately brightened. All I needed was that jump-start.

Now, if I could only hang onto this! I'd like to be able to keep that smile and share it with the people I meet. That's how God's love is shared and spread. And that's how I stay happy as well.

# Gratitude

*"Be joyful always; pray continually; give thanks in all circumstances, for this is God's will for you in Christ Jesus." (1 Thessalonians 5:16–18)*

SOME OF MY best days have been when I've opened my eyes in the morning and, without thinking, uttered a quiet but joyous, "Thank you, God." I can't help it. On such days, usually when I'm on a bit of a high, these words come naturally. Even when it rains, I feel brightness inside me. My smile comes easily.

Lately I've begun waking with Psalm 118:24 on my mind. I sing the hymn we sang in the church I used to attend, a hymn I loved. *"This is the day the Lord has made; let us rejoice and be glad in it."* That verse fills me with joy. I take such pleasure in it, I even say it when I wake up from an afternoon nap.

I'm glad my friends love me no matter what because they must think me weird when I call them and open the conversation with this verse. But they've come to understand me, and I think they're happy to be reminded. Our phone visit immediately takes on a cheerful tone. We laugh.

I was surprised recently to discover that the Bible has something to say about this. Ephesians 5:19–20 advises us to: *"Speak to one another with psalms, hymns, and spiritual songs. Sing and make music in your heart to the Lord, always giving thanks to God the Father for everything, in the name of our Lord Jesus Christ."*

(Once I asked my psychiatrist if what I was doing was normal. He looked me in the eye and said, "No, Marja, it isn't." It's good to have friends who accept me as I am, even when I act abnormally.)

With a little effort, we can learn to see the good in everything and be grateful. As I've matured, I've learned there is a bright side to every situation. Going through countless periods of ups and downs has helped me understand much about life. I don't thank God for the pain, but I do thank God for the compassion it has taught me. I understand others in ways I wouldn't if life had been easier. I am also grateful to God for giving me such a great appreciation for what it means to be well.

At the time I studied my hospital records and discovered my six-month stay there could have been avoided, I was angry. But my anger gradually changed to gratitude when I had time to digest this new information. I realized the past is gone, and I am thankful for having such a good life today. My hospital experience, though traumatic, did not damage me. The pain helped refine me, as in the "refining fire" the Bible talks about in Malachi 3:2–3. It helped make me who I am.

132

Erwin McManus, lead pastor of the Mosaic Congregation in Los Angeles, said: "Gratitude is the only thing that heals you from bitterness. Bitterness causes you to focus on the past. The person who focuses on the future is a person who lives with hope." How true I've found that to be in my own life!

There is much I have to be thankful for. I know that the gratitude I feel keeps me healthy. It helps me cope with the pain I struggle with so often.

# Addictions

I MUST CONFESS, over the years I have felt quietly haughty. I used to think I would never become addicted to alcohol. I had too much control to allow such a thing to happen to me.

So far I haven't had any more problems with addiction than an obsession with writing faxes to a good friend years ago. We exchanged letters daily, sometimes more than once a day. If I didn't receive a return fax within a day or so, my anxiety level became unbearable. I had a real problem.

I haven't come close to being addicted to alcohol or drugs. In fact, I so dislike the wooziness I feel when I drink wine that I seldom do. Until recently, I drank the occasional glass of beer, but only to quench my thirst in the summertime.

Awhile ago, I drank beer to settle my irritability. It helped me feel more mellow and at peace. My medication wasn't helping me, so I self-medicated. In the following days, I was again tempted to have beer to revisit that feeling. I needed to settle my body's restlessness and tenseness. Then it became clear to me that even I, a "good" Christian, could one day come under alcohol's control if I weren't careful.

I now understand why addictions are such a common problem for individuals with bipolar disorder. I can empathize with people who become trapped in addiction's clutches. I also understand how doubly important it is for people like me to remain close to

God, who will provide me with peace. When I feel the urge to self-medicate, turning to God helps.

# First Impressions

MY 94-YEAR-OLD mother-in-law has collected a great amount of jewelry over her long life, though she has never been rich. She has a favorite piece that she has worn frequently over the past four years. It is an amber pendant that some of us gave her for her ninetieth birthday.

Although it is attractive, I've often wondered why it is so special to her. A year ago, we gave her an agate pendant, a delicate, honey-colored piece, which we thought was quite beautiful. But I haven't yet seen her wear it.

When I think back to the occasions when she opened each of these gifts, I think I may have hit on at least part of the answer. The amber necklace came packaged in an expensive-looking, velvet case from a jewelry store. That made an immediate impression on her.

The agate pendant, on the other hand, came in a nondescript box, the only thing I could find to wrap it in at the time. With the wonderful honesty that comes with old age, she did not hide that she wasn't overly impressed.

First impressions count, sad but true. How I present myself to the world can make all the difference to how others see me. Many people I meet are aware that I have a mental disorder. If they aren't, they soon find out because I have made it public knowledge. This makes it especially important for me to dress well. I want to be looked on with respect.

When people first meet me, I want them to be interested in me long enough to find out what's inside me. Dressing attractively brings a bonus. When I dress well, I feel better too. I face the world with more confidence.

# A Busy Octopus

AT CHRISTMAS TIME, there is an abundance of wonderful food constantly set before us. Most of us overeat. Similarly, when I am a little high and see the colorful array of offerings life has for me, I want it all. I don't want to waste any opportunity. I could do photography projects, organize an event for the church or put together yet another recipe book. I become greedy, not for material things, but for the chance to partake in every lovely activity and challenge I think of. I race from one thing to another.

A couple of years ago, I set up a child photography business. It is only part-time, but I can get quite busy. I also have a passion for spreading awareness about mental health issues, which has led me to approach the media and even take on a large project like this book. I end up making commitments, many of them. I also need to devote time to an aging mother and mother-in-law. It all adds up.

My bipolar disorder pushes me to be creative, especially when my mood is high. Being creative is a good thing, but it can get one into hot water. I dream up ideas, often too many to manage at one time. Everything I want to do seems possible. I can't conceive of not being able to cope. My imagination is keen, and I become super-ambitious. During these periods, I accomplish a great deal. My life becomes complex, and a snowball effect occurs. My creative work makes me high, and being high causes me to take on even more work. Hypomania threatens to turn into mania.

It's often after such a high that depression descends on me. Then I'm in deep trouble, saddled with the mountain of responsibilities I had so enthusiastically built for myself. The obligations quickly seem impossible to fulfill. Making dinner and doing dishes look like insurmountable tasks. How then could I possibly do an intensive photo session or give a one-hour talk? I wish there were an easy way off the roller coaster. At times like these, I'd rather die than have to tell people I can't fulfill my commitments.

# Pacing Myself: The Challenge

THE ANSWER IS to pace myself, but that is a tough thing to do. In fact, it seems to be almost impossible. When I'm well, with my mood stable, I can't imagine anything could go wrong. I can't imagine a time will come when the things I'm working on could become unmanageable. As my mood rises to a hypomanic state, I begin to feel I can do everything. Ideas develop, and I believe I simply must carry them out. One idea builds on another. I can't hold myself back.

On top of this, I have a big sense of responsibility. I want to step in and help out wherever I see a need. Soon, I'm overwhelmed. All too often, I'm brought to tears, wondering how I could possibly do everything God has called me to do. I struggle to decide where I should focus my energy. Everything seems important.

I need to use the gift of photography God has given me. Finding clients is important if I am to continue what I love to do and what I feel I'm meant to do.

I need to continue taking care of my household and my mother and mother-in-law. I am the primary caregiver for both of them.

I want to enjoy the friends I've come to love so much. I want to spend time with them and support them when they need me.

I feel the need to raise awareness about mental health issues. This is a passion, without which I would not be the person I am. I want to write; I want to speak.

I want to establish faith-based peer support groups for individuals with mood disorders.

I need to finish writing this book to help others who are dealing with bipolar disorder.

But all of this is a lot to ask of myself. I am a very busy octopus. Why did God give me so much that I need to do and love to do? It's overwhelming!

# Then How Should I Live?

A LINE FROM Rudyard Kipling's poem *If* comes to mind: *"If you can trust yourself when all men doubt you, but make allowance for their doubting too."*

I have learned I must live confidently, yet recognizing my limitations. I want to and need to live authentically, expressing in all honesty who I am. Sometimes I live exuberantly; other times I'm reserved. Or I'm totally down. I often wonder, which of these am I, really?

I try to make friends that are close enough so I can be honest with them about my disorder. In turn, I would hope these friends would be honest with me when they start seeing me do more than what is reasonable for one person. It annoys me to hear the warning that I'm overdoing things. Many times I will not listen. Yet I do appreciate they care, and I do *try* to listen.

In the past few weeks, I've been exuberant, rather high. When I'm like this, I can handle more than the average person. I sleep only six hours per night, going to bed around 10:30 p.m. and getting up between 4:00 and 5:00 a.m. I work and play at a fast pace.

The trouble is I can't maintain this pace forever. Eventually I need to come down. The result is often depression. During years of less effective medication, my high mood sometimes went right off the page. I would then become manic or psychotic.

So, how can a person like me, someone who thrives on being a reliable contributor to her community, take on responsibilities with a clear conscience? I can never be sure my mood will be stable enough to fulfill my commitments. Yet there is so much work I want to do! There is so much I'm capable of! This is my quandary.

One answer is to limit the amount of work I commit to doing for others. If I limit most of what I do to personal projects, work I do for myself rather than for others, I'm not in as great a danger of letting people down. But I *like* doing things for others! I want to serve.

137

# An Opportunity Lost

IN 1988, I was offered the honored position of official photographer for the British Columbia Festival of the Arts. I hadn't asked for this job. The organizing committee had seen a spread of my photographs in our local newspaper. It featured black and white candids of young dancers backstage at a dance competition. The photos captured the girls' nervous excitement as they awaited their turn to dance. The stage lights lit their eager faces as they peeked between the curtains at what was happening on stage. Some dancers, dressed in their tutus, their hair swept back in a bun, revealed a sense of boredom as they leaned against a wall.

This was the kind of work the Festival of the Arts was looking for; this was the kind of work that excited me. We proceeded to negotiate a contract. I was thrilled.

It wasn't long, however, before I realized I couldn't go ahead with the work. How could I know whether I'd be well enough to work during the festival? In those days, my medication was not as effective as it is now. I was not as stable as I am today. How could I guarantee several months ahead that I would be sufficiently healthy during the time of the festival?

The festival committee tried to persuade me not to give up the job. But my conscience would not allow me to make the commitment. It was a sad time for me.

# An Opportunity Taken

THIS YEAR, I was asked to give a presentation on candid child photography at a major photography conference. This was also an honor. But once more, I struggled with the question of whether I should accept the invitation. Could I responsibly accept? I had been having problems for a while, and there was a distinct possibility that I might not be well enough at the time of the conference.

And yet, how could I turn down such an opportunity? Was it healthy to live in constant fear of failure? I knew I would do a good job of giving the workshop if I were well. How sorry I would be if I refused to speak and then found myself perfectly strong and able at the time of the conference! Don't many people battle with health conditions periodically? Was my situation really so different?

These questions led me to accept the invitation after all. I wrote the organizers telling them of my eagerness to give the presentation. But I included the following proviso at the end of my letter: "I should tell you that I have some health issues that crop up once in a while. Do you have some back-up programs in reserve should a speaker fall ill?"

I want to have a full life. I want the opportunity to offer the best I can give. Now I've learned there are ways I can trust myself while making allowance for doubt as well.

As it turned out, I was well at the time of the conference. I was proud of my presentation, and it was well received. I'm glad I went ahead with it.

*Chapter 8*

# FINDING SUPPORT

## My Need for Support

L ONG AGO I learned I could not live my life without other people's support. No one can, no matter how healthy. But for someone like me, who has recurring difficulties that affect how my mind works, this is probably even more so. What compounds the problem for many is that they don't want, or can't afford, to admit having a bipolar disorder. Stigma prevents them from searching for, and accepting, the support of friends.

I count myself fortunate to have had the courage to make my mental health problems public. Having written my personal story means my life is an open book—literally. I find support in many places. My friends have come to understand me because I hide nothing. I am honest about my weaknesses. In fact, I make it my business to educate people I meet whenever they show an interest. I sincerely wish others could find greater freedom to be open as I have been. One day, hopefully, this would be true for more people.

The burden of dealing with my symptoms would be much greater than they are today if I didn't have the understanding I need from family, friends, church and mental health agencies and professionals. If I didn't have my faith and all these people to support me, the rich life I live would not be possible.

# A Husband's Support

I WROTE IN an earlier chapter of the wonderful partnership I have with my husband, Wes. We have been married since 1969 and have been through many ups and downs together. I'm fortunate to have someone like him, someone who has never given up on me no matter how sick I have been at times.

Wes does not step in to help overly quickly when I have troubles. I have to ask him when I need help with the dishes or cooking supper. I find it a bit humiliating to have to do that. I'd much rather be well and not have to ask for such help. But the extent to which he has both helped me and held back in helping me have made me strong. I have learned to be independent and try to do as much as I possibly can on my own. Yet I know I can count on Wes should I really need him.

# Help with Dinner

I LOOKED AT the recipe, planning what I would need to do to prepare the evening meal. But as I read, I became discouraged. Whatever energy I had had faded. All I could do was go back to my easy chair in the living room and eat half a bag of potato chips.

I hadn't been this down for a long time. In fact, my mood had been elevated so long that I had almost come to believe depression was gone forever. Yet here I was, someone who loves to cook, feeling unable to put a few ingredients together for a simple casserole.

When Wes learned how badly I felt, he offered to do the cooking. I dragged myself out of the chair so I could show him what I had planned to make. But once in the kitchen with him by my side, I thought I might as well do one or two things to help. Having him with me encouraged me to try.

While I grated the mozzarella cheese, Wes put on a pot of water to boil and measured out eight ounces of rotini. Once I had finished grating the cheese, I decided to gather some of the other ingredients he would need. I measured out the parmesan cheese and the sour cream. Then I chopped the basil leaves.

Gradually my energy returned, more than I had thought possible half an hour earlier. Some of the heaviness lifted. What a relief to know I was functioning and still able to contribute! I stayed in the kitchen and helped to complete the meal. The casserole was a tasty one: pasta with a creamy cheese sauce, combined with mixed vegetables and tuna. We both enjoyed it.

I'm grateful for the help Wes gave me that day. Without his support, supper would not have happened. I would have felt I had let him down. I would have finished the entire bag of potato chips. How the guilt would have added to my misery!

This joint project provided one of the building blocks for my recovery.

## Wes's Support During a High

*I've done it again! And Wes didn't see it coming. He, my supporter, my caregiver when I'm not well, agreed with my plans to have his mom stay with us for a few days. This would have piled one more thing on top of all I'm doing. Even Wes, who understands the pattern of my hypomania—how it can lead to acute instability, how it can threaten my sanity—even he missed the danger.*

*It seemed like such a good idea. Yet, he forgot about the many other things I am doing. He forgot my doctor pre-scribed an extra anti-psychotic because I have become so overwhelmed. He forgot that only yesterday, I had to seek the help of a counselor to put some order in my life—to help me find a way of coping with an overwhelming number of activities. Fortunately for both of us, Mom decided she would rather stay at the home. We missed having her but knew it was for the best.*

*Currently I'm looking after the needs of my mom and mother-in-law, a small photography business, writing this book, running a household, keeping up with friendships and attending church and Bible study, camera club and writers' group meetings. A lot of stuff!*

*But I don't blame Wes for not seeing what is happening. Others, no matter how close to me, often miss problems as they develop. Along with me, they see each of my new ideas (and I get many ideas) as a good one. It's not easy supporting me when I'm on a high. And even when Wes or a friend does recognize a problem, it can be difficult—if not impossible—to convince me I'm building a stack of blocks that will tumble if I don't stop and rest.*

*I'm fortunate God gave me a husband who loves me enough to have stuck by me, even during the times when my towers have tumbled. I love him dearly and will do all I can to help him have faith in my ability to be well.*

## Giving and Receiving Support

*"...live in harmony with one another; be sympathetic, love as brothers, be compassionate and humble." (1 Peter 3:8)*

EVERYONE KNOWS HOW important it is to have the support of friends. But I have found if I want supportive friends, I must be prepared to support them as well. Support is a two-way street; the health of any relationship depends on it. It is good for me to help someone instead of always being on the receiving end. I don't want to be set apart from other people; I don't always want to be the needy one. I'd much rather be strong, ready to help.

I have had a problem for much of my life: my own interests are uppermost in my mind when I share visits with friends. A few months ago, I read a passage in Rick Warren's book, *The Purpose Driven Life*. Warren wrote about how God is an example of "other-centeredness." That term impressed me deeply. I decided I needed to strive to be less self-centered. This is not easy for me; I do it poorly. At times, my own projects are so exciting I have trouble listening to others. At other times, I'm so consumed with the pain of depression, all I can talk about is my misery. When I do listen, I become less self-absorbed.

I'm learning that when I show an interest in other people's lives, I'm supported almost as much as if we were talking about me. By caring about others, I benefit. My friends and I connect on a more equal level. When I'm aware of what's happening in my friends' lives, I'm better able to help. But often I'm not aware.

Often I seem to be on the receiving end. I have two marvelous Christian friends who have seen me through many bad times. I'm thankful to them and love them for it, but I wish I could do something for them; our friendship seems to be far too one-sided. There appears to be little I can give back. They are strong, never in need as I am. Our conversations all too often turn to me, what I'm doing, what I might be going through. They don't tell me their troubles as much as I tell them mine. Maybe it's my fault; maybe I don't listen.

I feel ashamed of needing my friends so much. I worry about leaning too heavily on them—of being too self-absorbed. It would be easier, more gratifying, to be a giver rather than a receiver. Jesus said, *"It is more blessed to give than to receive."* (Acts 20:35b) I pray that I will in some way be able to give back.

Perhaps one day I will learn how to support others as these good friends have supported me. I think that's beginning to happen.

Sometime, maybe these friends will feel comfortable enough to allow me to help them when *they* are in need. To know that I could give what they have given me would give me joy. I could be God's hands for them as well.

# Sharing Out of Brokenness

*"To the weak I became weak, to win the weak. I have become all things to all men so that by all possible means I might save some. I do all this for the sake of the gospel, that I may share in its blessings." (1 Corinthians 9:22–23)*

FRIENDS WHO UNDERSTAND what it means to be in emotional turmoil are special to me. I have a friend, whom I'll call Cynthia, who has periods of depression, as I do. She is one of the best people to talk to when I'm going through bad times. We're not close friends; in fact, we haven't known each other very long. She's much younger, and we've haven't done much together. Nevertheless, we know that in this aspect of our lives, we have much in common.

When I need to talk, Cynthia is a good person to call. If I'm feeling bad, hearing that she has had a similar experience makes me feel better. We can connect with each other because we suffer from the same problems. Sometimes we alert each other to Bible verses we've found helpful. By sharing how God works in our lives, we find comfort.

In past years, quite a few troubled individuals have opened up to me. They know I'm a safe person to talk to because I've been open about my own struggles. They know I will understand. I feel blessed that they are willing to confide in me and trust me, giving me an opportunity to share what has helped me live my life. These relationships are special. I can take the minus in my life, this mood disorder, and turn it into a plus.

# An Employer's Support

A NUMBER OF key individuals in my life have encouraged me in the past. One of the greatest of these was Bert Cowan, the office manager of B.C. Industries (BCI), a drafting and engineering equipment and supply business. I worked for this company for a total of seven years during a period when I was first learning to live with my disorder.

I had worked in that office during the summer months before I first became sick and was hospitalized. When I was discharged from the hospital, I went back and asked if I could work without pay until I was well enough to become a useful employee again. Bert agreed to take me on. Working was tough, but I improved every day. After two weeks, he called me into his office and gave me a small paycheck, something I hadn't expected. It felt good to be valued in such a tangible way.

A few months later, I was re-admitted to hospital. Bert came to visit, bringing along a huge cluster of grapes. I'll never forget how much I enjoyed that visit. I was very sick and had not been able to communicate well, but the time he spent with me was meaningful. As we munched the sweet, juicy grapes, we talked. He treated me with respect and understanding.

Only in recent months, when I studied my medical records from those hospital days, did I discover that Bert had offered to let me come back to work at that point. If the hospital had discharged me, as a private psychiatrist recommended, I would have had my job back. Looking back at the situation as revealed in my records, I realize I could have asked for release myself. I didn't need to wait for the hospital to discharge me because I had freely sought this hospitalization; I had not been committed against my will. But I was too young and confused to understand that. So I remained institutionalized for another six months.

Eventually, I went back to BCI. Although I struggled with symptoms, my years there were valuable years of recovery. Despite my diagnosis of schizophrenia (an incorrect one), Bert gave me many opportunities to learn and gain confidence. He gave me some of the most challenging and interesting jobs in the office.

My main position was invoice clerk. But once I was given an assistant, I had opportunities to try out many other duties. I often filled in when other employees went on holiday. I tried shipping and purchasing and even worked as office supervisor.

My fondest memory was that of updating the BCI catalog, a binder showing the products the business carried. When it became outdated, I researched the new products that should be included, found illustrations and wrote descriptions. A secretarial service down the hall typed the descriptions in the format I specified. I then arranged the new items on the huge paste-up sheets and glued them in. Other items simply needed updated pictures and perhaps a new description. The project was huge, sometimes unwieldy. New pages had to be added, and old pages needed shifting. It was a puzzle to be solved, and I enjoyed the creative process.

The catalog project introduced me to publishing. For the first time, I saw endless creative possibilities. When I have something to share, I can create a single item, and—in a process I still see as magical—have it printed. One item, easily multiplied to share with many. While at BCI, I published my first booklet, *Marja's Favorite Recipes*. I had thirty copies printed, enough to give away at Christmas to family and friends. Was I ever thrilled to be able to do that!

Bert Cowan did something special for me. By trusting me with so much, he encouraged me and helped me build my self-esteem. How many employers, even today, would give a person with mental illness the opportunities he gave me? I was, at the time, far from finding God. But I believe God was looking out for me, even then, by bringing Bert into my life.

# Church Support

I HAVE FOUND support in all facets of my life: at home and camera club, from friends and professionals. But I have probably received the most support from my church.

Over the past eighteen years, I have belonged to two church families. Each has contributed to my welfare and growth. I don't know if I would have begun speaking out about mental health issues if it weren't for them and the faith they encouraged in me. The worship services inspired my growth as a follower of Christ, and the people, my sisters and brothers in the faith, seldom failed in their love and support.

Most of the members of my first church family, Cliff Avenue United Church in Burnaby, were aware that I had severe mental health issues. They had read about it in my writing for the *Vancouver Sun* newspaper and a church publication, *Fellowship Magazine*. They were my best fans when *Riding the Roller Coaster* was published.

In spite of my mental health challenges, they included me wholeheartedly in everything I wanted to be a part of. They valued me as a member of the congregation. In the fertile ground of this church community, the seed of my faith was planted and grew, little by little. I found ample sunshine there.

Dale Cuming, the pastor at one time, was especially encouraging. He was always ready to listen when I needed to talk and gave me things to read. When I received an award for raising mental health awareness, he made a big deal of it and admired the plaque. He, together with a ministry group I belonged to, surprised me with a bouquet of flowers, making me feel truly special. When *Riding the Roller Coaster* came out, he was proud of me and showed the book to many people. Though they moved away years ago, Dale and his wife, Marlene, remain good friends today.

I took on many roles at Cliff Avenue Church. The encouragement I received to contribute was probably my best form of support. I created posters expressing my faith and posters of church events. I worked in the nursery and visited those too sick or too old to come to church. I advertised the fall fair for many years, coordinated the publication of a church cookbook, and created inspirational Easter and Christmas cards and booklets. For a while, I was an elder. I served coffee and I served communion. I received lots of hugs and gave lots of hugs.

148

A couple of years ago, God led me to Brentwood Park Alliance Church. This is an evangelical church, quite different from what I had become accustomed to, but a better reflection of the faith environment I had grown up in. I came to love the worship times, with the lively songs, the keyboard, drums, guitar and bass. I received a warm welcome and quickly began to feel at home.

This congregation is a younger one. I'm one of the older members of the ladies' Bible study group. Before long, I began to feel younger and learned that I was able to get along with people of many ages.

I enjoyed Pastor Don's sermons, forty-five minutes long, but riveting. They fed me richly. The focus at Brentwood Park Church is to spread the Gospel beyond the walls of the building. I had never thought I would have a zeal for mission work. With time, I surprised myself. I found out I had a lot I wanted to share. One of the results is this book. I don't think it would have come about had God not led me to this congregation.

## Part of God's Family

*"...in Christ we who are many form one body, and each member belongs to all the others." (Romans 12:5)*

DURING TIMES OF depression, I often have difficulty feeling God's presence. I know God is there, but I can't connect. He feels distant. One of the best things about having friends who follow Christ is that God can touch me and show his love through their support. A hug and words of encouragement or affirmation help. Sometimes a friend will lend practical help with a meal or shopping. One friend goes for occasional walks with me. It is important to have someone who will spend time with me and listen to what I need to say to unburden.

My ladies' Bible study group has been particularly helpful. By studying scripture and learning how to apply it to our lives, we share as only women can.

Soon after I joined the group, I revealed my mental health problems. I had to. It was either that or be artificial or untruthful. In our discussions, we all had to be candid. I'm a candid person by nature and could never have deceived them. This was a safe place to disclose my struggles. Everything discussed was confidential.

I am often in danger of focusing too much on myself. This group gave me the perfect place to unlearn this tendency. I learned to listen better and hear what others were dealing with. My own troubles came into perspective. Through talking with these friends and praying and caring for each other, we became close. Our love for each other grew. We were like family. We "...carry each other's burdens, and in this way...fulfill the law of Christ." (Galatians 6:2)

# The Lonely Person in the Pew

I LOVE PEOPLE very much and can show it when I'm well. I like to talk with them and share my life with them. I laugh with them when they're happy and feel sad with them when they're troubled. I'm a friendly person at church.

But when I'm depressed, I sometimes sit at the back of the church, not wanting to be hemmed in by other worshippers. Here, it is less obvious to others when I cry or don't stand to sing the songs. I can only sit and receive; I don't have much to give. I let my friends worship for me.

Even so, my time at church helps me. Many of the songs echo my feelings. In the safety of the back pew, I wait patiently for God to speak to me.

When I'm depressed, communicating with others becomes difficult. I want to talk, I want to be friendly, but it's hard. Instead, I sit quietly, only watching and listening. I long for some caring words.

Sadly, people who don't know me then think I'm not a friendly person. They can't see who I am inside or know my feelings.

That has made me wonder: How many individuals who seem unfriendly and unapproachable are actually feeling down and in need of someone's attention? A friendly smile and a warm handshake might be exactly what they need to restore them, at least temporarily. Everyone needs to sense that someone cares. And often those who seem least lovable are most in need of love.

# Healing Touch

*"Blessed are those who mourn, for they will be comforted."*
*(Matthew 5:4)*

THE LAST TIME I was in hospital, I was in extreme distress during my first few days. I was having breakfast on the ward, trying my hardest to fight back tears and not having much success. The chaplain was in the room talking to someone, not paying much attention to me, but she noticed my tears. From behind, she placed her hand encouragingly on my shoulder.

I broke down, no longer from the pain, but from release of pain. Through her touch, I felt God's presence and comfort. When I talked to her about it later, she didn't even remember the occasion. The memory stays with me as a sweet reminder of love expressed by someone who cared. This simple warm touch, by a compassionate woman, worked wonders.

During another unstable period of my life, I was at a church service and the words of a hymn made me cry inconsolably. I didn't know what to do. I wanted to leave but was hemmed in by people on both sides. My friend's daughter, only sixteen years old at the time, put her arm around me and gently asked if I'd like to go downstairs. She led me from the pew and took me to a quiet room in the basement. A few minutes later, her mom came down and spent time with me.

On another occasion, I sat in church during a song while everyone else stood. I wasn't upset, only tired—perhaps a bit down. A friend in the pew behind me placed her hands on my shoulders as she sang. Her hands felt warm. I felt cared for. This is another memory I will forever treasure.

# A Special Friend

*"But I have stilled and quieted my soul; like a weaned child with its mother, like a weaned child is my soul within me."*
*(Psalm131:2)*

SOON AFTER I moved to Brentwood Park Church, the leader of my Bible study group there befriended me. I couldn't have found a more caring person to help me through the rough times I faced. Helen exemplifies what true Christian support can be. She was, and still is, a treasure.

Helen cared enough to study the symptoms of my disorder. No one else in my life has done that as conscientiously as she did. She read *Riding the Roller Coaster* in an effort to understand me. When my husband was out of town and I was going through a series of mood swings, she was there for me. She wanted to know exactly what she could do. She checked in on me often, either by phone or email, and was ready to talk whenever I needed it. We did things together as I tried to recover. She even joined me in a session with my psychiatrist.

To know someone is aware of my trouble, is praying for me and following up with occasional phone calls helps a great deal. I feel cared for. I don't need to worry as much about myself. I'm able to relax and feel free to get on with things. I do my chores, and I'm better able to meet my commitments. Thank God for a friend like that!

# "If All Men Count with You..."

"...BUT NONE TOO MUCH." Those lines from Rudyard Kipling's poem *If* have always puzzled me. How could anyone be too important in my life? How could anyone be too good a friend?

With age has come a touch of wisdom. I can see how relying on one person can make me dependent and her feel stifled. Friends have their lives to live and others to support. They have worries of their own. Demanding the attention of one person can cause her to burn out.

I'm learning to develop a variety of friends to go to when I need to talk. I'm finding each has something to offer me. Spending time with different people enriches my life. It gives me a broader perspective on things.

Over coffee or on the telephone, we share what's happening. As we get to know each other, we share what's in our hearts. This is particularly true of my Christian friends. My church's small group is especially important to me. Through studying the Bible together, we have developed a bond that makes us like sisters. We connect.

# When Life Seemed Impossible

I FELT I didn't want to—in fact, I couldn't possibly—continue. I dreaded every day. The responsibilities I had taken on frightened me. How could I possibly manage? I was fed up with the ups and downs, tired of not being able to count on myself. I was ashamed of my weakness and overwhelming despair.

Most of my shame was because I had been open at Bible study that morning. I had said things I now regretted. Nothing that would hurt anyone. I had talked about the struggles I had been having with pride—pride that was separating me from sensing God's presence. Yet now I felt ashamed of having shared this.

It would have been easy to get off this roller coaster. I no longer wanted to live. I had a plan to take some pills, pills that would easily put me to sleep. I would never have to wake up again. This seemed the only alternative. Better than admitting I couldn't live up to my commitments. Better than telling someone I had to back out of the publicity work I had promised to do for a conference, work that was important to me. I would be so ashamed!

These thoughts rolled around in my mind as I leaned back on the pillows. A reasonable future seemed impossible. I couldn't see past my misery. I called Helen.

# A Friend in Need...

I'D HAD MANY stimulating conversations with Helen about what God meant to me. I was able to talk to her about my beliefs and my doubts. I respected her and how she worked to spread the Gospel, how she made new people feel welcome in our church. I always felt comfortable with her and had come to love her very much.

When Helen heard what I was going through, she said, "I'm coming over for a cup of coffee. I'll be there in a bit." I felt instantly reassured: here was a friend who cared enough to drop everything for me. She didn't *ask* if she could come over. She *told* me she was coming. I had no opportunity to refuse. That gave me great comfort.

As we sat at the kitchen table drinking our coffee, she encouraged me and quieted my worries about how I had come across at Bible study. She told me how she had prayed on the drive to my house, asking to be God's presence for me. And she was.

She asked me about my thoughts of taking my life and whether I had made plans. She impressed upon me how important my writing was and how she believed God was using me. She said, "Marja, I love you and I will always love you, no matter what you do or say." How that touched me!

Through this compassionate friend, I experienced God's love in a way I never had before. Many times, I had talked about God's love and written about it for others, but I had never sensed it so deeply. I had never known this certainty and the joy it brought me. For the first time in my life, I not only *knew* about God's love for me, I felt God's arms around me. I felt God would never let me go.

This visit, lasting no more than an hour, was the impetus I needed to turn myself around. I gradually moved away from the negative thinking, and my mood normalized. Since then, I've experienced depression, but suicidal thoughts—at the time of writing two years later—have not been part of it. I realize the desire to die may return; it's a common symptom of my disorder. If it does, I will try to remember what Paul said: *"...that neither death nor life, neither angels nor demons, neither the present nor the future, nor any powers, neither height nor depth, nor anything else in all creation, will be able to separate us from the love of God that is in Christ Jesus our Lord."* (Romans 8:38–39)

When God feels distant, I will strive to remember this doesn't mean God isn't there. God is always with me. I will see God in my friends. *"If I go up to the heavens, you are there; if I make my bed in the depths, you are there...your hand will guide me, your right hand will hold me fast."* (Psalm 139:8 & 10)

## Wishing for an End

I AM NOT often suicidal. My nature is to be positive, to try to see the best in everything. Yet, that doesn't protect me from depression or even the occasional wish to die. Some time ago, I again found myself in the depths, even making plans for my way out of life. I did not think of heaven or of hell. All I could think of was how I wanted to stop the suffering, suffering that seemed always destined to return. I could not remember how it felt to be happy, nor could I imagine ever feeling happy again.

155

But I asked myself, "What if Jesus had succumbed so quickly to the pain he faced? What if he had decided not to go to the cross? Where would we be?"

Because of who he was, he could not have refused the cross. In Philippians 2:8, Paul wrote that though Jesus was human, *"he humbled himself and became obedient to death—even death on a cross!"*

He did not *want* to suffer the pain. *"My Father,"* he prayed, *"if it is possible, may this cup be taken from me."* Yet more than that, he wanted to obey. *"Yet not as I will, but as you will."* (Matthew 26:39b) He knew his sacrifice would mean we would live. It was humanly possible for him to refuse the cross, but he didn't. His love for us was far too great.

I needed to look to Jesus as an example of how I should live. Even if I have periods of great trouble, I can hope these will one day be for the good. I can't be Jesus, but I can try to obey. If I can hold on to my desire to be like him, this will be possible. I need to stay close to God.

My musings continued: "How can I throw away the life God gave me? God must have meant me to use it for something. It would be such a sin to walk away from that!"

I found consolation in Paul's second letter to the Corinthian Christians. He wrote, *"He comforts us in all our troubles so that we can comfort others...As you share in suffering, you will also share God's comfort."* (2 Corinthians 1:4, 7 NLT)

"Maybe there's a reason for what I'm going through," I mused. Considering that my pain might have some value, that it might even be useful for something, encouraged me. "If I can continue thinking of this as God's assignment for me in life; if I can see this suffering as something I need to fulfill my calling; if I can keep my faith and rest by trusting in God, if I can do all these things, then I can survive—and even grow! I can share with others what I've gone through and discovered. I want to help others learn how to cope with their troubles."

I did grow. God did comfort me. I do share.

156

# My Ultimate Source of Support

*...God has said, "Never will I leave you; never will I forsake you." (Hebrews 13:5)*

MY WORST MOMENTS are occasional feelings of abandonment. I usually experience these at night. I have a sense of doom, a chilly emptiness. There is nothing to hold on to. No hugs are tight enough to take away my sense of disconnectedness. I'm filled with a huge sense of insecurity. I cannot sleep.

I don't know where these feelings come from. Are they part of my bipolar disorder, or are they the result of multiple separations from family due to illness and hospital stays when I was young? Could they be Satan's work? But the cause doesn't really matter, does it? All I know is that at times such as these I need to go to my Bible. I need to pray. I need Jesus.

Some of the worst suffering Jesus endured was the sense of abandonment he felt in the Garden of Gethsemane as he tried to come to terms with the cross he knew he had to face. While he was in emotional anguish, his closest friends slept. Even Jesus, the Son of God, needed support from his earthly friends. "Can't you understand that I need you?" was in essence what he cried out to his disciples as they wiped the sleep from their eyes. They had no idea what he was dealing with. Neither do my earthly friends when I'm in need. How can one person possibly understand what is happening in the mind of another? Only Jesus understands. He knows pain.

I can't fathom how horrifying it must have been to deal with abandonment in the face of having wrists and feet nailed to a cross and being left to die a slow, excruciating death. I'm sure the cross would not have been as painful had he known there were friends below, expressing love and concern. But his friends deserted him. The people for whom he was dying mocked and ridiculed him. *"He saved others, but he can't save himself!...Let him come down now from the cross, and we will believe in him!"* (Matthew 27:42) Eventually he was even abandoned by his Father in heaven. *"My God, my God, why have you forsaken me?"* (Matthew 27:46) he cried.

When I'm in pain, I have Christ I to go to. Jesus did not have a Christ to turn to. He had to deal with the agony of the cross on his own, without friends and, for a time, even without God. He bore the weight entirely alone.

His great love for us made Jesus willing to walk to the cross. Love allowed him to endure the torture. Even as he hung there, wracked by physical pain, loneliness and humiliation—all because of us!—he begged his heavenly Father to forgive us: *"Father, forgive them, for they do not know what they are doing."* (Luke 23:34) he prayed. He went through all of this because he knew we would then have everlasting life. Because of his sacrifice, I don't have to suffer as much as I otherwise would.

When I need to talk to someone and no one is home, or when phone lines are busy, Jesus is always there, waiting for me. When I feel I've been deserted, I search my Bible and pray, and Jesus hears my cries. I can pour out my heart to him, and he fully understands.

I cover myself warmly, lay my head on the pillow and sleep peacefully once more. I know that I'm taken care of.

Thank you, Jesus!

# I Discover a Gift

I READ THE two previous pieces at a Good Friday service in 2006. Sharing my thoughts and feelings at such an appropriate time was a privilege. I was surprised to receive a good response from the congregation. Several individuals came to me in the weeks afterward to share some of the pain they had experienced in their own lives. We were connecting in a special way.

This reminds me of what happened to Patch Adams in the film of the same name. It tells the true story of Dr. Hunter Adams. While he is a patient in a psychiatric hospital, Patch discovers he has an ability to connect to the people there. He learns to understand his severely disturbed roommate—to see the person behind the ill-ness—and manages to help him through his problems. Not only does this delight him, it makes him a well man.

Patch eagerly tells his doctor he has become well and needs to leave the hospital. "I connected to another human being. I want to do more of that. I want to learn about people. I want to help them with their troubles. I want to really listen to people."

I have been feeling a similar eagerness lately. In recent months, I have learned to be a better listener. I am more interested in those I meet. Like Patch Adams, I'm also able to connect well with peo-ple who are in trouble. I have found out that if I want to help peo-ple, I need to let them know I understand them. I need to listen with compassion and love. I don't have to have answers. How freeing it is to know that's all I have to do to make a difference in people's lives!

In his devotional book, *Unto the Hills*, Billy Graham quotes a person as saying, "To have suffered much is like knowing many languages. It gives the sufferer access to many more people." I sense that happening in my own life. I feel as if I know many lan-guages. I can relate to a wide variety of people. And I feel as Patch Adams did: excited!

I'm happy when I've connected with someone and am able to help her find a way to deal with her problems. She becomes a per-son I can spend time with. We can relate deeply to each other. I am confident that she will share in my pain when I'm in trouble, too. When either of us is in need, we will remember each other and offer up a quick prayer.

When I am able to connect with others and help them, I be-come like Patch Adams—well and strong.

## *Living Room*

ONLY MONTHS AFTER the Good Friday service, God gave me an idea that wouldn't stay quiet. I wanted to start a faith-based support group for people with mood disorders. I knew there was a need. Several people in our church, including me, could use a place to talk about their struggles. Secular support groups were readily available, but participants do not always feel comfortable talking about God. For those who believe in Jesus, discussing faith issues is important in dealing with emotional problems.

Don Dyck, our pastor, liked the idea, and we set the wheels in motion. The process took time. Where would we meet? How would we let people know about it? Would it be for our church alone, or would we advertise in the community? What would a meeting look like? Who would facilitate the group?

The last person I thought of to lead the group was me. I could not see myself doing anything like that. Yet, as our plans progressed, I received the courage to take charge of the project and decided I would like to try facilitating. I felt very nervous at first, but gradually I had a change of heart. A few months later, when we were ready to have our first meeting, I was eager to lead, confident I could do so. This kind of courage, so new to me, was not of my own making. The church was praying for me and for the group. Don and many in the congregation were excited about the program and supported it wholeheartedly. God was definitely with us in this.

We called the group *Living Room*, a name coined by Dr. John Toews, a psychiatrist and author of *No Longer Alone: Mental Health and the Church*. Dr. Toews is a proponent of better church support for people with mental illness and helped inspire the organization of our group.

*Living Room* became an outreach project in partnership with the Mood Disorders Association of BC (MDA), a secular organization that trained us how to facilitate. Pastor Don would not let me start without a co-facilitator. We found Janice, a great support for me and someone I could not do without.

We advertised in MDA's newsletter, as well as the local community newspapers. The calls trickled in at a steady pace until four months later we had twenty people on our list. Many others called as well, people who may join us in the future. At the time of writing, each meeting is drawing an average of twelve people.

Though I focus on the participants, I mention my own struggles at group meetings. This tells them I am one of them. When I talk about my feelings, others are encouraged to talk about theirs. We study scripture and share our suffering, always relieved to discover that others understand.

Relationships built on authentic sharing of our vulnerabilities become strong. Because we have all suffered, we have compassion for each other. We share a common language. When the participants believe in God and talk about how God works in their lives, the strength of our bond grows. Not only do we share similar emotional problems, we encourage each other's faith. We share God's love with each other.

An amazing thing happens to me as a result of leading these meetings. Though we talk about sad things, I feel uplifted when I go home, emotionally and spiritually. After meetings, I pray, thanking God for this gift. It is hard to describe the joy I have found in this work.

My desire to give support rather than always being on the receiving end has been met in *Living Room*. I'm helping others deal with their problems. To give *is* to receive. The more support I give, the less I need to go to others for help. I feel stronger, happier and more whole than I ever have before.

When I think back to the needy person I used to be, I'm amazed where God has taken me.

# PART FOUR:
## LIVING FOR GOD

*Chapter 9*

# LIVING
# CREATIVELY

## Famous Creative People

THE MYSTERIOUS CONNECTION between madness and genius has long intrigued me as it has intrigued society in general. Many famous people who have bipolar disorder have reached high goals in spite of their condition—or maybe because of it. The Internet carries long lists of individuals with a variety of accomplishments who are believed to have lived with this disease. Those lists give me comfort and encouragement. They reinforce my belief that this disease does not have to hold me back from leading a rich life.

Kay Redfield Jamison, PhD, long-time psychologist at Johns Hopkins University in Baltimore, is a researcher and writer responsible for much of today's understanding about the relationship between creativity and bipolar disorder. Her book, *Touched with Fire: Manic-Depressive Illness and the Artistic Temperament*, is a well-known treatise exploring this connection. In her introduction she writes, "Recent research strongly suggests that, compared with the general population, writers and artists show a vastly disproportionate rate of manic-depressive or depressive illness; clearly, however, not all (not even most) writers and artists suffer from major mood disorders."[10]

The terms "manic depression" and "bipolar disorder" have only been around during modern times. Even forty years ago, when I became sick, my symptoms were misinterpreted and not recognized as bipolar. The medical community has a much better understanding now. The letters and biographies of historic, famous people show that this disorder was present in many. George Frederic Handel's records show he probably suffered from it. He wrote his two-hour-and-twenty-minute oratorio, Messiah, in twenty-five days during what was most likely a hypomanic episode. About this work he wrote, "Whether I was in my body or out of my body as I wrote it I know not. God knows."

Lord Brain, a British neurologist, was one of the first to diagnose manic depression in author Charles Dickens when he spoke of Dickens' "general mood of elation, associated with hyperactivity and broken by short recurrent periods of depression."[11] D. Jablow Hershman and Julian Lieb, MD, in their book, *The Key to Genius: Manic Depression and the Creative Life*, describe Dickens this way:

> Dickens's brain, more than that of most manics, was a machine that ran day and night. It would not allow him to escape into sleep and often drove him for many dark hours through the streets of whatever city he happened to be visiting. He was extraordinarily hyperactive. He did not work, he overworked: the Dickens oeuvre includes books, innumerable short stories, articles, speeches, a play and an operetta. He also edited magazines, gave lectures, went on reading tours and acted in and directed fifteen plays. He was active on behalf of others, raising funds for orphaned children, setting up a home for 'fallen women,' and working out plans for improved sanitation in tenement areas. This list is not exhaustive.[12]

Former British Prime Minister Winston Churchill is also believed to have had bipolar disorder. Dr. Ronald Fieve, in his book entitled *Moodswing*, told this story:

> In the early 1960's I had the good fortune to meet and talk one evening with Churchill's only son, Randolph, the writer and journalist who died in 1968....He talked about his father's serious and prolonged depressions. Randolph also told me his father had had periods of high energy when he was forceful, driving, tireless, and in need of very little sleep. At those times, Winston seemed to be able to achieve whatever he wished, to conquer any impossible situation, to succeed brilliantly as a writer, politician, warrior, or prime minister.[13]

Incidentally, Churchill was also interested in art, frequently painting as a hobby.

A book called *The Price of Greatness: Resolving the Creativity and Madness Controversy* gives the results of a ten-year study done by Arnold M. Ludwig, looking at the lives of 1,004 men and women prominent in a variety of fields, including art, music, science, sports, politics and business. He studied these people by reading 2,200 biographies and concluded that "members of the various creative arts professions, as a whole, display higher rates of various emotional disorders than those in other professions..." Between 59 percent and 77 percent of the artists, writers and musicians he studied suffered mental illness, while only 18 percent to 29 percent of the other professionals did.[14]

# Creativity as the Result of Moods

*"You turned my wailing into dancing; you removed my sackcloth and clothed me with joy." (Psalm 30:11)*

KING DAVID, THE author of many psalms, knew strong moods. He sang about the great contrasts he experienced in life: fear and trust; weeping and rejoicing; the pit and the rock. Our well-loved Psalms would be hard to imagine without the strong expressions of joy and sadness he describes so well. David's mood fluctuations made him a great psalmist. As Thomas Carlyle said, "A great soul...alternates between the highest and the lowest depth."

Strong moods produce the strong feelings so important to making vibrant pieces of art. These moods are particularly apparent in those who live with bipolar disorder. Mania, hypomania and depression cause a great ebb and flow of emotions that can spur individuals to imaginative pursuits. Of course, not all who have intense feelings have mental disorders.

Though depression is vacuous and sterile of productivity, it has proven to be part of many artists' experience. No one gets much done while he's depressed. Even getting out of bed is difficult at such times. Yet that mood, though painful, has value in that it provides a deep understanding of life. This makes it an important ingredient in what creative people do. Artists with bipolar disorder and also those with unipolar depression develop creative passions because of insights they acquire while they are down. For many, depression provides fodder, without which they would not have such inspiration. When their mood swings upward again, they have much to work with.

The great contrast in the moods I experience, the steep highs and deep lows, supplies me with the sensitivity I have toward others. This is one reason I've become a photographer. I can spend an hour at a time focusing my lens on a baby's myriad expressions. By recording how young children respond to the world around them, I can convey feelings I myself have experienced in my life. Each child is different; each has a different set of emotions. With each of my young subjects comes an opportunity to express some different aspect of myself.

Researchers, including Jamison, feel that a person experiencing mania is able to think more creatively. In fact, one of the diagnostic criteria for mania is "sharpened and unusually creative thinking and increased productivity."[15] Jamison identifies a number of qualities of hypomania and mania that artists with the disorder experience. Amongst them are "fierce energy, high mood, and quick intelligence; a sense of the visionary and the grand; a restless and feverish temperament."[16] These qualities are part of my make-up when that mood is upon me.

Hypomanic phases have caused me to embark on many projects: publishing note cards, plaques, bookmarks, inspirational booklets and cookbooks. Intense feelings have motivated me to work hard to create photographs that express clearly what I want to say. In a single evening of work in the darkroom, I fill the wastebasket with dozens of prints that do not live up to my standard.

Big projects don't frighten me. Most of the time, I have the energy and I enjoy the challenge. I have organized parties for a hundred people. I have planned and coordinated workshops and support groups for people with mood disorders. When I've done publicity work for my church and other organizations, I tend to get carried away and will not rest until I've explored every possible avenue. If I'm not engaged in an interesting challenge, I soon get bored.

I constantly come up with ideas I need to talk to my friends about. My long emails express my philosophy, reactions to books I've read and plans I want to carry out. It's hard to go for long without communicating with my friends, often to the point of excess. I have a lot inside me, and it must come out. This impassioned spirit is with me a good deal of the time, even when I'm not clinically high. It has become part of who I am. Sometimes, this creative drive becomes overly strong and I carry it too far. If I were not taking medication, I would become manic.

Though my forty-year roller coaster ride has not been an easy one, much good has come out of it. Frequent low moods have supplied me with empathy toward the thousands who suffer as I do. Most are not as fortunate as I have been; many don't receive the support they should. I recognize the great need for a better understanding about mental health issues. Frequent high moods feed my hope that I can build a better awareness. Bipolar disorder has supplied me with passion, energy and perseverance. Without this disease, I might not possess such a high degree of determination to do my part in creating a better world.

## Appreciating the Good Stuff

*"...whatever is true, whatever is noble, whatever is right, whatever is pure, whatever is lovely, whatever is admirable—if anything is excellent or praiseworthy—think about such things." (Philippians 4:8)*

PHOTOGRAPHY HAS LONG helped me stay happy and feel fulfilled. It has been a healing outlet for my emotions. It helps me focus on some of the best the world has to offer. Photography has taught me to see.

Even when my camera is out of reach, some of my most elated moments come during my walks as I look closely at the flowers in my neighbors' gardens. Appreciating a cluster of dew-covered crocuses in early spring fills me with an indescribable joy. I quietly utter a brief prayer—"Thank you, God."—and how my heart dances within me!

Wes and I have been avid photographers since we were married in 1969. We've photographed landscapes, seascapes and cityscapes. We've spent countless hours with flowers in nature and flowers in gardens. We've studied them closely and captured them on film. We have learned to see everything around us with an appreciative eye. Through our images, we share with others the delight we take in the world. This sharing gives us great satisfaction.

I had a friend, a fellow photographer named Lilie, who also loved what she saw in this way. Someone once said of her, "God made the world for Lilie to photograph." In spite of great problems with cancer, she never tired of recording the outdoor splendor she appreciated so much.

I have fond memories of going with her on a short photography trip. She remarked on every group of daisies we passed on the side of the highway. She insisted on stopping at every photogenic location we happened upon. With insatiable joy, she shared her appreciation for beauty. All of us fellow photographers loved her dearly for this. Through her superb pictures, her heart touched ours.

The sicker Lilie became, the harder she worked to make photographs. She could not bear to let what she witnessed be forgotten. As she lay dying on her hospital bed, she and her sister May looked at slides from the last trip they took together. Toward the end, Lilie became too tired to go on. As she lay back on her pillow, she smiled, saying, "The fun was in the taking, anyway."

Whenever I pass a group of daisies, I think of Lilie and her passionate spirit. I'll never forget how her creative work energized her and made her happy. Her photographic escapades gave her strength to continue through situations that would have driven less inspired souls to bed. Taking beautiful pictures was healing to her.

Lilie was physically sick, but appreciating and being thankful for the good things around us can help with all kinds of problems, including psychological ones. Although I'm not a Lilie, although my problems are not of a physical nature, I have found this to be true for me as well.

# A Creative Life

*"For we are God's workmanship, created in Christ Jesus to do good works, which God prepared in advance for us to do." (Ephesians 2:10)*

I'VE HEARD, THOUGH I can't substantiate it, that people who have not been creative in the past often become creative after their first manic episode. This is what happened to me. I was not creative until after I first became sick forty years ago. Then I came to enjoy making things and making things happen. Even when I'm not in an elevated hypomanic state, being creative has become a habit for me. I thrive on it.

In 1985, I wrote and published *The Camper's Cookbook*. During our camping holidays, I tired of the basic, boring cooking I was doing on our two-burner Coleman stove. I longed for more interesting recipes, but with no oven and only two burners—only one of them truly hot—I was limited in what I could do. Realizing that other campers must be experiencing the same problem, I tested recipes and created this recipe book specifically for the purpose. I enjoyed the project immensely and learned much about the publishing process. Over the next four years, I sold 4,000 copies.

My love of candid child photography, combined with a desire to tell stories about what it is to be a child, has led me to creating photo books about them. Clients hire me to spend time with their children and design a "storybook" with the photos, combining them with words. I then have the book printed and bound in linen, giving parents an alternative to the traditional album. The creative process that comes into play is an exciting one because the results are always a surprise. I don't plan what to shoot or what story I want to tell. Instead, I allow things to happen. Whatever the child chooses to do determines the direction the project will take, making plenty of room for surprises to happen. That is true adventure.

Because of what I live with, I recognize the need to erase the stigma that keeps those with mental health issues from getting the support and care they require. I also want to share what I have learned about living with bipolar disorder. Both of these concerns have encouraged me to write articles and books about mental health issues.

And so I putter each day on my wide variety of activities: cooking, photographing and writing. Sometimes I work on a publishing project; sometimes I plan an event; sometimes I do something simple like knitting to relieve stress. There are few days when I'm not working on some creative venture.

# Mom's Work

*"Give, and it will be given to you. A good measure, pressed down shaken together and running over will be poured into your lap. For with the measure you use, it will be measured to you." (Luke 6:38)*

WHEN MY MOTHER was young, she was the unhealthiest of all her ten brothers and sisters. Constantly sick with what we today believe might have been rheumatoid arthritis, she did not take part in many of the games her brothers and sisters played. When my sister, Ineke, and I were children, she was sick much of the time. We often had to stay with friends or relatives because Mom was too sick to look after us or she was in hospital.

But today, at the age of ninety-three, she has outlived all her siblings. There are, of course, health concerns, but she is able to live on her own in a self-contained suite. With the help of her walker, she goes to the dining room in her facility for lunch and dinner. She likes to attend all the programs available to the residents: church services, music performances and the daily coffee hour. She never misses watching the Friday night carpet bowling tournament in the lounge.

Mom spends every free hour she has crocheting and knitting. It's something she seldom puts down. She lives for this work. And almost all of it is done for the benefit of patients in the care-facility part of the complex she lives in. I'm sure what is helping Mom live so long is the love of her work and the knowledge that it's being used for the good of others.

One of her favorite projects these days is crocheting small afghans. She has made an endless abundance of these. Along with other craftspeople, she donates these to the care facility. Whenever new clients come to the home, they receive an afghan big enough to cover their lap. Mom follows no fixed pattern. Each time she makes a new one, she uses her imagination to decide on colors and design. That's a big part of the fun. When I make my daily phone call, Mom enjoys describing the design and colors of the current piece she's making. She is doing what she loves to do; she is doing what God put in her heart to do.

For many years, Mom made plastic canvas embroidery, creating a great variety of items, among them jewelry boxes, bookmarks, coasters and Christmas decorations. Whenever her home had a craft sale, Mom was given a long table to herself. Each year, she sold several hundred dollars' worth and donated everything to the home. She felt good about that, and rightly so. The Bible says, *"It is more blessed to give than to receive."* (Acts 20:35b) Mom is proof of that.

Creative activity helps keep a person happy, healthy and vibrant. Mom has found that out, and so have I.

## Managing my Creative Urges

FORTUNATELY, THE MEDICATION I've taken for many years has pretty well removed full-blown mania and psychosis from my symptom list. At one time, with excessive creativity I became increasingly unable to communicate. The words I spoke could not keep up with my rapid thinking. I no longer worry about this. As long as I stay on my medication and it keeps working for me, I will be fine. Nevertheless, I have to be careful. I should never count on my current treatment to always be the right one. My body's requirements can change; my life situation can change. I must never take my present good health for granted.

Today, my problems tend to be limited to occasional depression and hypomania. I'm fortunate enough to be on non-sedative pills. They have brought with them frequent extended periods of mild highs, or hypomania. This is not all bad: I often have the creativity and sharpness that comes with being high. I have to try persistently not to overdo things. I need to live responsibly. The higher I become, the more easily I could drop into depression. Even now, mania and psychosis are not impossibilities.

I often stop to assess whether I'm trying to do more than God intends for me. My mood sometimes threatens to become like a snowball rolling down a hill. The more I do, the more I want to do. I become increasingly consumed with work. Eventually, the ball could grow so big no one would be capable of rolling it, let alone lift it. My challenge is to prevent this from happening.

Currently, my main focus is to help people who suffer with some kind of emotional problem. I write and speak and also plan to work toward forming more faith-based mood-disorder support groups like the one I started at my church. Throw into the mix my effort to keep up my photography, socialize with friends and care for home and family, and I have a lot to handle. I often have to battle periods of stress. Lately, I've kept handy something Thomas R. Kelly wrote: "In our love for people are we to be excitedly hurried, sweeping all men and tasks into our loving concern? No, that is God's function. But He, working within us, portions out His vast concern into bundles, and lays on each of us our portion...He is at the helm. And when our little day is done we lie down quietly in peace, for all is well."[17]

This reminder helps me rest and reflect that I'm just one little person who needs to do only one little thing at a time.

## Developing Empathy

*"He comes alongside us when we go through hard times, and before you know it, he brings us alongside someone else who is going through hard times so that we can be there for that person just as God was there for us." (2 Corinthians 1:4, MSG)*

I CLEARLY REMEMBER a day when, as a preschooler, I awoke from a nap to find my mother gone. Although it was mid-afternoon, the windows were covered with heavy drapes, shutting out the bright sunshine. In the darkness, I called out, "Mama, Mama!" but no answer came. Our home was dead quiet. A great fear grew inside me.

I went to the window, parted the curtains slightly and looked down onto the street. Strangers walked along the sidewalk. They all looked like bad people. Their faces appeared angry. I panicked, thinking they had taken my mama away.

Bursting into tears, I called out again, crying "Mama! Mama!" I was certain that Mama had been kidnapped, certain she was gone forever. It was lonely in that dark room. Our friendly home did not feel friendly anymore. I felt abandoned, threatened by the bad people outside.

Mom did come back. Thinking I would sleep longer than I did, she had gone for a short visit with the neighbor in the flat across from ours. I was, of course, extremely relieved. Yet, this event remains securely fastened in my memory. I will never forget it.

Many traumatic experiences, this being the first I remember, have played a big part in making me who I am today and in the empathy I have developed toward others. This empathy forms the basis of much of the creative work I do.

As a youngster, separation from the rest of my family was often necessary. When my mother was sick, a frequent occurrence, my sister, Ineke, and I stayed at the homes of family and friends. I was also often sick and spent much time in hospitals. I've already recounted my six-week experiences away from home at the ages of seven, eight and nine. As a sensitive child, these absences from the family were painful.

In the hospitals, as well as in the "colonies" in the country, I yearned for individual attention. It is said that loneliness is most common when a person is in the presence of many. This is so true. I remember clearly a brief period when one nurse, to whom I became attached, spent extra time with me. That meant a lot to me.

But it was short-lived. She was not able to keep it up, and I was once more left alone, this time lonelier than ever.

My time in the mental hospital as a young adult was no better. I have a clear understanding of what institutionalization feels like. I can only imagine what institutionalization without hope of release must be like. I deeply sympathize with those who have to endure that.

## Ministering to Others

MY HOBBY OF producing hand-made Easter and Christmas booklets for seniors is one product of the empathy I've developed toward others who struggle. I create these especially for those in hospitals and care facilities. I love challenges, and these booklets give me a great opportunity to brighten the lives of those who suffer from material losses, loss of physical or mental well-being, as well as loss of independence.

As I work on each booklet, I try to think of what would make me feel better if I were an older person reading it. I try to share God's love with them by helping them with their loneliness, their need to remember happier times, to laugh, to be entertained, to be encouraged. I try to fill their need to connect with God through prayer and scripture. I usually work with a volunteer artist, someone who also gets a thrill from using her work for such a project.

In ministering to others' needs, I minister to my own needs. The feelings institutionalized people experience are still recessed in my own memory. As I work, I identify with them and I work hard, careful to get the right emotional balance. I love this work and hope to do much more of it. I have produced about fourteen such booklets in the past and know they have been appreciated.

In all the creative work I've undertaken and all the energy I've put into it, I have received the greatest blessing. Each booklet has provided me with healing and joy. The work I have taken on to promote understanding about mental health issues has also been a gift to me. I feel my own life is in better control. I'm healthier. As I begin each day, I know what I'm living for. I know what God made me to do.

# Desire to Help Others

THE MANY KINDS of dysfunction I have suffered have taught me much about what it means to be misunderstood and shunned. My awkwardness and withdrawn nature as a teen, psychosis as a young adult, battles with depression and out-of-control highs have helped me understand others who suffer. I am able to put myself in the shoes of those who are down and out or different from the average person. Having survived, I want to help others survive.

My desire to influence change is aroused when I see the many homeless and realize it is commonly estimated that 25 percent to 33 percent of them suffer from mental disorders. A large percentage of those with severe mental disorders become addicted to drugs and alcohol in an effort to cope with their illness. Those with these co-occurring disorders are the most likely to end up homeless.

I am sad and angry about a world that allows these individuals to flounder. They have an illness, an illness that is not their fault. They should not have to suffer without care and support.

When I think of these homeless individuals, I think to myself, "That could be me." If God hadn't been so good to me, if I weren't so fortunate in the amount of support I've received, and if I weren't taking medication, I would not be sitting so comfortably in my home right now.

After my son was born, I tried to work at a number of jobs but didn't succeed. Like the homeless, I, too, would be struggling to stay alive if I didn't have Wes's financial support. I understand the health problems that have driven so many to where they are today. The empathy I feel is a huge part of what I am and what drives me to do as much as I can. I want to build a better understanding of what it means to have a mental disorder.

## A Time to Make Things

*As I write this, I'm mildly depressed and feel a pull to make something, especially something that will be of use to someone else besides me. I'm thinking once more of producing some kind of inspirational booklet for older people who might be lonely or depressed as I am. I want to share with them the hope I have found in the Lord. In the process, I know I will be uplifted.*

*My writing is not working out very well right now, and I need to find something else to pour myself into, at least temporarily. Perhaps I could make use of my photographs in some way and combine them with Bible verses, poems and stories. I long to touch people's hearts and prompt joy, gratitude, worship, prayer and laughter. Trying to fill others' needs is healing.*

*On my refrigerator door, I have a quote from Frederick Buechner. It has become my guide. I often look at it and never fail to be inspired. He said, "The place God calls you to is the place where your deep gladness and the world's deep hunger meet."*

WHEN I BECOME mildly depressed, I need to try and make something. Being creative is therapeutic and gives me satisfaction. My moods are easier to endure. The positive activity helps heal my negative thinking and supplies me with energy. Creative activities have long been a source of joy when I am stable; they're a source of comfort when I am down. When I'm slightly up, ideas tumble out one after another, especially in the form of writing.

Long ago, at a time when I suffered from frequent bouts of depression, I searched for a new creative project every time I felt myself going down. Making things became my lifeline. Eventually, as I grew in the faith, I learned to see this creativity as a gift from God, one that helps me survive.

My creative endeavors supply me with purpose for my day-to-day life. The purpose changes from time to time. As I complete one project, another one always waits in the wings. In spite of the frequent health difficulties I face, this makes my life a happy one. The Bible says that when a person is happy in his work, *"he seldom reflects on the days of his life, because God keeps him occupied with gladness of heart."* (Ecclesiastes 5:20) This is the way it is for me.

Although my life isn't easy, I'm fortunate in that I've heard God call me to many different places, always depending on where my mood happens to be. Sometimes God calls me to photograph, sometimes to write, sometimes to cook and entertain friends, sometimes to fold bulletins for the church. I can always fill a need somewhere, no matter where I happen to be emotionally. In filling the needs of others, I fill my own needs.

# Inspiration

THOUGH IT'S TRUE that *"it's more blessed to give than to receive,"* we need to receive on a regular basis if we are to give. If we're going to feed, we have to be fed. A starving individual can't do much good in supplying others' needs. We need inspiration; we need a source from which to draw our creative energy.

Periodically, I take time out to pore over the photographic books in my collection. Seeing the work of other photographers excites me. I study the images, trying to identify why they move me. Why do I enjoy them so much? What is the photographer trying to tell me? What can I learn to help me with my own photography?

On nature walks along the lake near our neighborhood, I study the skunk cabbage growing profusely in the ditches. I enjoy the grasses and always find it a challenge to make a photograph that will express the harmony I see as they bend elegantly in unison. Sometimes, I tuck my camera into its case and simply wander down the path, drinking deeply from what I see growing around me. I feel a sense of awe and gratitude.

When I need a break from the stress of my work, I frequently stop what I'm doing, put on one of my favorite CDs and sit back. Surrounding myself with music fills me up, especially when I'm home alone. Sometimes, I like sad music to mirror a quiet, reflective mood. Other times, I listen to one of the lively groups from the Canadian Maritimes to reflect my cheerfulness. I join in, singing and clapping. Music will dance with me when I'm up, or it will cry with me, providing comfort, when I'm down. Music helps me let go of what is inside.

Feeding on God's creation and my fellow man's creation enriches my life. I am grateful for how it fills me, how it restores my soul.

## The Creative Drive

*"Do what is right and good in the Lord's sight, so that it may go well with you..." (Deuteronomy 6:18)*

CREATIVE WORK HAS become a driving force I can't live without. I've learned that going for extended periods of time without a project pulls me down and threatens depression. I need to keep active, yet not overly so. This is how I find my greatest satisfaction and happiness.

I love to read, yet I'm not truly happy unless I can balance this "ingoing" activity with a creative, or outgoing, activity. The joy all my hobbies have given me is immense. Making things has helped me share who I am and what I love with others. This has been true of all I do, whether it's an art like photography or a craft like cross-stitching pictures or knitting a sweater.

Sometimes, I become overly active. Then I might feel my inner engines revving, yet they don't take me anywhere. That's a sign that it's time to relax, read a book, watch a movie or spend time with friends. After a brief rest, I'm ready to get to work again.

Writer Brenda Ueland describes the value of creativity for our well-being in a way that expresses exactly what it has done for me: "Why should we all use our creative power...? Because there is nothing that makes people so generous, joyful, lively, bold and compassionate, so indifferent to fighting and the accumulation of objects and money."[18]

# God's Presence in my Work

MUCH GOOD ART is God-inspired—awe-inspired. I have found this to be true in my work. Years ago, before I went to church or even knew I was searching for God, I sensed God's presence in my photography. This understanding came to me as a revelation. I was producing some particularly good images and felt there was something else at work here. I thought to myself, "These photographs could not possibly have come solely from my efforts."

This phenomenon may seem strange to those who do not yet believe in someone greater than themselves. For most of my life, I would have snickered at such an idea as well. Today, I know it to be true.

This knowledge can't be proven by human means. It is a truth of the spirit that can only be understood by a heart standing open to receive, as mine was at that time. It takes a heart that is willing to forget about personal pride and surrender to God's way. It takes the presence of the Holy Spirit.

In her book, *The Artist's Way*, Julia Cameron wrote, "When we open ourselves to exploring our creativity, we open ourselves to God; good orderly direction."[19] I would reverse the order of this statement. In my experience, when I open myself to God, I open myself to exploring creativity. It starts with God.

I'm not the only person who has sensed God in her work. Many creative individuals will attest to this. William Blake wrote, "I myself do nothing. The Holy Spirit accomplishes all through me." And Johannes Brahms said, "Straightaway the ideas flow in upon me, directly from God." Giacomo Puccini said this about his opera, Madame Butterfly: "The music of this opera was dictated to me by God; I was merely instrumental in putting it on paper and communicating it to the public."

When I allow myself to be led by God, I create out of the good I experience. I reveal God's glory by sharing the best his world has to offer.

# In God's Image

*"Be imitators of God, therefore, as dearly loved children and live a life of love." (Ephesians 5:1)*

THE BIBLE SAYS that God, the greatest creator of all, made us in his image. God also made *us* to be creators. We can continue the work God began by using the talents we've received.

When I make a photograph I'm happy with, one I have put all my sensitivity and skill into, I often stand back, look at it, breathe deeply and whisper to myself, "It is good. Thank you, Lord." In a small way, I sense what God must have felt as God completed each day's work making the world we live in. The Bible says, *"God saw all that he had made, and it was very good."* (Genesis 1:21) That statement expresses a heart that is filled up, a heart full of joy.

I create photographs of subjects that mean a lot to me. If I didn't feel that way about them, I would not bother. When I make a photograph that expresses what I feel and share it with others, it becomes truly meaningful to me. I become attached to the piece of work I've made.

I'm sure God must feel the same about all he created, especially when God created us. That understanding makes me want to be the best I can be. I want to please my heavenly Father. I want to use all the talents and skills God has given me. It makes me happy to do so.

I use my writing as a tool to do God's work helping those who suffer with mental illness. I use my photography to worship and glorify God's name. My photographs are the songs I offer up to God.

By using the gifts God gave me, I can't help but do what Paul wrote in Philippians 4:8 (NLT): *"Fix your thoughts on what is true and honorable and right. Think about things that are pure and lovely and admirable. Think about things that are excellent and worthy of praise."* I want to express the joy I've found in living for God. I want to be there with God, helping to create a better world—a more beautiful world, a happier world, a world better fed in every way.

Animals don't have the ability or desire to create in the way we humans do. They don't make sofas, tables and chairs. They don't build cars, trains or airplanes, telephones or computers. They don't paint or sculpt. They would never be able to make medication to help themselves live healthier lives.

When I stop to think about it, my mind boggles at the extent to which God has made us creators. I realize how important it is to use the skills God gives us to serve our world.

## Creating in Obedience to God

*"For God is working in you, giving you the desire to obey him and the power to do what pleases him." (Philippians 2:13)*

WHEN I FEEL the God-given urge to write down a thought, to look for a new knitting pattern or to lie down in a field of daisies with my camera in hand, I must respond. I often hear God's still small voice in the early morning placing ideas in my heart. I've learned to obey this voice, to accept God's leading. If I think about it for a while and the idea does not go away, I know I must respond.

When I feel the urge to remodel the bathroom, to plant a garden or to cook a meal for friends, I see it as a call from God. God made me a person who enjoys causing things to happen. I get up each day excited. The more I respond to the urge, the more I'm inspired to do.

I hear from many who want to be creative in some way. Yet, all too often, their courage fails them. They get trapped by other things they feel they need to do, things that may not be important. They get trapped into doing "safer" things. It is much easier to be on the receiving end of creativity than it is to give. I know what it's like: I've been there. But when I was there, I was not happy.

While preparing to write this book, I read widely to understand how people deal with life issues. I wanted to explore what in my own life helped me deal with my frequent mood swings. But all too often, this research became an excuse not to write. It was much easier to be fed than to feed.

When I let the Spirit produce fruit by acting on the urges, I can create wonderful things—but only with God's help. In John 15:5, Jesus said, *"I am the vine; you are the branches. If a man remains in me and I in him, he will bear much fruit; apart from me you can do nothing."*

## My River

*"For out of the overflow of the heart the mouth speaks."*
*(Matthew 12:34)*

I'M A LETTER writer, at times far too much so. When I have an idea, I need to share it. When a Bible verse speaks strongly to me or puzzles me, I need to discuss it. When something exciting happens in my life, I can't keep it to myself. I write when I'm happy, when I'm excited, when I'm hurt. The river inside me must flow.

What's in my heart must come out. That's the kind of person God made me to be.

I'm a communicator by nature. This has helped me as a photographer and writer. I have been known to email friends almost daily, and my letters have been long. I felt guilty about bothering one friend, though she didn't complain. I wondered if I might be overdoing it: she was a busy person with many friends.

Recently, I resolved this problem by creating a web log. I've made friends with other bloggers who have bipolar disorder. Now, I can write all I want, knowing it will be read by people who understand me, people whose rivers are as full as mine. My letter writing no longer flows out of control.

## It's for Everyone

*"Whoever believes in me...streams of living water will flow from within him." (John 7:38)*

GOD GIVES EACH of us unique and special gifts. Not everyone can be an artist, but every one of us can be creative. Everyone has something to contribute, something to give to others. Having something to give is a gift.

I have found freedom in being true to myself, in not looking at how others do things or lead their lives. Being open to where God leads me, and not holding back, fulfills me.

Creative living fully charges me and makes me feel alive. As I give life to a project, I am empowered; I feel in control. If it weren't for me, what I create would not exist. I sense the significance of my life.

We don't have to be a Mozart or Michelangelo to be creative. Instead of becoming a musician or artist, we can find ways to be imaginative or resourceful in the things we do. Creativity is important in every human endeavor: in work and play; in career and home life; in relationships with friends and family and people in the community. Creative living can include all fields of activity: supporting the sick or poor, growing a garden, teaching. It means finding ways to help others. It means making the world a better place.

By its very nature, being creative should have passion at the center. Devotion to the work and the people it serves is vital. This means surrendering to God's calling, finding our unique purpose, the one God planned for us. *"For I know the plans I have for you, declares the Lord..."* (Jeremiah 29:11)

As I know all too well, our society can trap us and hold us back from being the fully alive individuals we can be. Being creative takes energy and courage. Yet, all too often, we are tempted to be consumers instead of creators. We can easily become stagnant, with life flowing in but not out.

God intended us to be rivers, fed by streams from the mountain tops. By responding to God's call, we can pour ourselves out—clear running water flowing through a thirsty land.

*Chapter 10*

# FINDING
# MEANING

## Searching for a Life of Value

NINE MONTHS IN a mental institution, followed by difficult years of recovery, affected me deeply. The loss of such a significant part of my life made me value wellness. I didn't want to waste any of it. I spent much time examining what my life should be. I often meditated on Rudyard Kipling's words in his poem, *If*: *"If you can keep your head when all about you are losing theirs and blaming it on you. If you can trust yourself when all men doubt you, but make allowance for their doubting too."* Kipling became my trusted guide for this chapter of my life.

After Wes and I were married in 1969, I worked full-time for a short while, but the stress of working all day while maintaining a household became too much. I suffered from relentless headaches. The office manager, Bert Cowan, agreed to let me work mornings only. Afternoons were gloriously all mine.

This new freedom was exactly what I needed. I was able to spend a couple of hours every afternoon working on needlework projects. I had time to experiment with new recipes. Creativity became a form of medicine for me. Making things with my hands was healing.

Those afternoons gave me important hours, hours to think about what I wanted out of life and what I wanted to give to my life. I did a lot of inner talking, especially on the countless occasions when I felt sorry for myself, thinking of the great difficulties I faced. And when my ruminating mind threatened to bring on the paralysis of depression, I would remember Kipling's poem: *"If you can dream—and not make dreams your master; if you can think—and not make thoughts your aim."* I learned to be a doer.

As I worked, I thought endlessly about what was important in life and how I would like to use my time. I decided to give instead of take; I wanted to make instead of use. I reached the conclusion that I wanted the world to be a better place after I died because I had been there. I felt a need to leave something of myself behind. Yes, I thought, I will create heirlooms, beautiful things to leave to my children, a record that I have lived and accomplished something. I intend to live a life of value. Life is too precious to waste. While I'm able, I must use my days as well as I can.

So my thoughts went, day after day. I encouraged myself, became angry with myself, struggled to hang on, tried to come to terms with the stigma. I filled my time working with colorful yarns and embroidery cotton. Whenever a low mood began to descend, I tried to ward it off with a new project.

I cross-stitched a large Dutch sampler with very fine stitches. In the center, I embroidered my initials and in the lower right corner, my name and the year it was made. My son and daughter-in-law will receive this after I die. It will be a way of leaving something beautiful behind, a little piece of my history, a way to prove that I have lived. This sampler still hangs on our kitchen wall.

I made a needlepoint version of Millet's famous painting, *The Gleaners*. I made petit point portraits of native Indian children. I taxed my eyes creating single-thread petit point roses to mount in small oval pendants. I undertook the huge task of crocheting a wool afghan in afghan stitch and then covering it with an intricate cross-stitched flower design. This piece I recently presented to my son and his new wife as a wedding gift.

All this work was fulfilling; it was comforting. But throughout, I struggled with my emotional balance. I had to work very hard to stay in control and to live the kind of life Kipling had prescribed for his son, even when I sometimes watched *"...the things I gave my life to broken"* and had to *"...stoop and build'em up with worn-out tools."*

Through these years, the poet's words buoyed me up: *"If you can fill the unforgiving minute with sixty seconds worth of distance run—yours is the Earth and everything that's in it, and—which is more—you'll be a Man, my son!"* His advice was fatherly. He understood true difficulties. He understood me.

# Finding Meaning

TO LEAD A life of meaning, we need to know that what we do and what we are matters. We need to know there's a reason for living. My search for meaning led me to create material items. That was all that was within my reach, emotionally, in those early years of my adult life. Going beyond this to a more mature view of life's purpose took years.

But at this time in my mid-twenties, I learned how to treat my life as a treasure, one I did not want to waste. Lord Chesterfield's words became how I lived: "Know the true value of time; snatch, seize and enjoy every moment of it. No idleness, no laziness, no procrastination; never put off till tomorrow what you can do today."

With so many wonderful projects to fill my time, I looked forward to each day. I gradually learned to believe more in myself and began the slow process of building self-esteem.

The Nazi death camp survivor, Viktor Frankl, saw how some of his fellow prisoners survived. He concluded that, "those who have a 'why' to live, can bear with almost any 'how'." Making things gave me a reason to fight the symptoms of my disorder. Being creative helped me survive and find happiness and fulfillment.

Twenty years later, when I began to follow Christ, my life took on much greater meaning. I began to see my purpose in less materialistic terms. Slowly but surely, I discovered different, more spiritual reasons for living. I ultimately learned that living for the good of other people made me happier than living for myself. I learned that loving God and others was more meaningful than anything else imaginable. My mental health became stronger. I gained the courage to do things I would never have believed possible for me.

But I had years of living to do before I reached that point.

# I Become a Publisher

WHEN I GOT married, I realized I would have to cook every day. To prevent this from becoming a chore, I decided to look on it as a hobby. I came to love looking for recipes and trying them out. I spoiled Wes by cooking something different every day of the month. We seldom went out for dinner.

One night when I couldn't sleep, an idea emerged to create a booklet of the best recipes I had discovered. At work, I had come to know a little about how books are put together. The thought of publishing my own collection of recipes excited me. I couldn't bear to lie there any longer. If I'm not going to sleep, I thought, I might as well get up and get to work. I couldn't wait.

And so, at three o'clock in the morning, I sat down at the dining room table with my father's old Remington and began typing recipes. A good thing Wes was a sound sleeper! If he heard the tapping of the typewriter, it didn't seem to bother him. He left me alone.

I had great fun planning, trying to include a variety of entrees and dessert items. I found illustrations and copied them with a fine felt pen. A photo of a chicken's feet sticking out of a large pot amused me. Though I wasn't a particularly good artist, I managed to draw a version for the section on poultry. I decided to head that chapter with the archaic word "fowl," but I misspelled the word as "foul." It wasn't until after the booklets had been printed that I made the discovery. That taught me how important it is to have someone proofread my work.

I remember how eager I was during the days I worked on this. I couldn't wait to get home from my morning at work so I could play with my project. Although making booklets of any kind is a common and easy thing to do nowadays, back in the sixties it was not something the average person did. This was a creative adventure.

When I finished my planning, typing, drawing, cutting and pasting up of all the elements, I took my handiwork to the print shop below the office where I worked. They made thirty copies, enough for me to give as Christmas presents to friends and relatives. My first cookbook was born.

Since then, I have self-published the full-size *Camper's Cookbook*; a family cookbook, *Around the Family Table*; and a church cookbook, *Come Cook with Us*. I also published the booklets, *Recipes for Seniors* and *Up Recipes for Down Times*, as well as inspirational booklets for seniors.

All these projects were wonderful, meaningful endeavors. They gave my life color. I shared something of myself that gave enjoyment to others.

## I Become a Photographer

ONLY MONTHS AFTER we were married, Wes and I joined a camera club, a club we still belong to. We were quickly caught up in making photographs for the monthly competitions. Each competition night, a judge from outside the club reviewed the images, gave points and made comments on each one. The critiques taught us what to look for if we wanted to create good photographs. Wes and I learned quickly. Soon we were winning awards.

Both of us became involved on the club executive. Although my self-esteem was low to begin with, I gained confidence as the years went on. I took on many positions in the club, even spending a year as president. I felt accepted there. Even when my mental health faltered, my friends at the club did not seem to think less of me.

Gradually, I became interested in child photography, making sixteen-by-twenty-inch black and white enlargements of my favorites. Though photographs of people did not commonly do well in competition, my portraits were well received. But it did not matter to me that I might have won more awards if my subject matter were different. I enjoyed this work.

I loved photographing young children at their most natural. Feeling a bit like a child myself, I could relate to them. I found the honesty with which they presented themselves beautiful and thought it important to preserve their candid moments. Child photography became one of my most enjoyable, rewarding endeavors.

## In Search of Fame

COMPETING WAS NOT enough. I wanted to see my pictures in print. Many of them were good editorial material. I found several markets in the US and was able to sell many. To see my pictures serve a useful purpose was satisfying.

Soon, I decided I wanted to be recognized for my photography. I wanted to make money. I wanted to be well known in a way that was more meaningful than receiving prizes at a camera club. I wanted my portraits of children to be accepted as an art form.

I had noticed that the local paper, *The Royal Columbian*, always publicized the art displays at the small *Place des Arts* public gallery close to our community. Perhaps I, too, could have a show, I thought. I, too, might have my picture in the paper. It would be a good step to becoming the recognized photographer I wanted to be. It was the *United Nations Year of the Child*, an excellent reason to have an exhibition of child photography.

I gathered some of my best images and made an appointment to see the curator. To my delight, she accepted my proposal for a show. A few months later, a picture of me standing in front of my photographs appeared prominently in *The Royal Columbian*. The show was publicized in several other publications as well. In addition, the cable television station produced a fifteen-minute documentary about my work. Soon after, I had a portfolio published in a national photo journal with a story about my work. I was on my way.

Because I received this attention, I was asked to sit on a panel at a photo conference. The discussion was about photography as an art form. I felt honored, because the other two panelists were highly regarded as artists. Here was I, sitting with these men, discussing such a grand topic!

Other one-woman shows followed. I was getting my way. I was receiving recognition. But it wasn't as much fun as I had hoped. It wasn't as meaningful as I had thought it would be. What's the point of all this? Who wants to buy photographs of other people's children? I sold almost no prints. I found out that, more than anything, I just wanted to produce good pictures. That's where the true joy lay. Gradually, I no longer considered it important to be famous.

Nevertheless, I wanted to earn some money—more than the little I received for editorial work. I yearned for some kind of tangible proof that my work had value. I craved proof of my own self-worth. Photography was more than a hobby; it was of ultimate importance to me. Photographing children was what I did best. I was incapable of enduring the stress of a full-time career. But I needed to be recognized for *something*.

## Giving My Best

MY NEEDLEWORK, COOKING, photography, as well as the other creative work I pursued, taught me that doing my best was of utmost importance if I were to be satisfied with myself. The more I gave myself to my work—and my play as well—the more pleasure it gave me.

Producing photographs for competitions trained me to seek perfection. Each time I worked in the darkroom, I filled the wastebasket with prints that were not good enough. Sometimes they needed more contrast; sometimes bright areas needed to be darkened; sometimes dark areas needed to be lightened. I scattered eight-by-ten-inch proofs around the kitchen and living room, living with them for days or weeks. This gave me time to determine whether they were worthy of enlarging further. Does the picture have anything to say? Is it strong enough to stand out? Is it worth preserving? Or is it simply too ordinary to warrant more attention?

For a couple of years, I freelanced for our local community newspaper. I spent a good deal of time at each assignment. Even after I had shot a lot of pictures, I hated to leave, thinking I might miss something important. I made every effort I could to produce the very best photo story possible. Long after other photojournalists had gone home, I would still be there, watching, waiting, shooting.

I learned perseverance, something that has followed me in other pursuits. I've found out that anything worth doing is worth doing well. I don't give up on it, as long as I have energy and as long as there is hope that I can create something special.

One evening, during the time I was working for the newspaper, I was a guest speaker at a photography club. As I showed my work, I discussed why I had taken the pictures and why they were important to me. One of the members asked me, "Do you let the newspaper have your best work?" He added, "I never let my best work go."

This comment has stuck with me. It reflects a way of thinking I can't understand. I give my best, because the harder I work at something, the more significance it will have—not only for me, but for others as well. What good is something excellent if it is hidden in a drawer for no one's eyes except my own? Everything I made was most meaningful to me when I could share it with others.

However, though I created many things, I often felt as though nothing was enough. Time and again, I asked myself, Is that all there is? The things I did seemed to lack sufficient purpose. I was never satisfied, not until years later, after I had turned to God.

## Out of Gratitude

ONCE I HAD found God and my spiritual journey had begun, my outlook on life quickly changed. My new discovery of how God loved me and had a purpose for my life gave me great joy. It filled me up.

Before that, my photographs had often expressed loneliness and emptiness: groupings of tall, dead grasses in the mist; abandoned playgrounds with slides and swings shrouded in dense fog; sad-looking children. These themes no longer interested me. I now yearned to create photographs expressing my gratitude for the new life I had found. I longed to express the love of God I had discovered. My children's portraits became less moody. I preferred photographing colorful flowers on bright days to roaming around in the fog. My work became a form of worship.

I learned from my Bible readings how God wanted me to love others as he loved me. This was my desire. I wanted to give to others what God had given me. I felt called to follow Jesus' model.

During my morning prayers, I asked God to fill me with his love and help me share it with others. God answered these prayers. All I had to do was ask. I was able to show love more easily. A new world gradually opened up to me. I became a more outgoing person, able to give, able to serve. I became active in the life of my Cliff Avenue Church, helping at the annual fall fair and church dinners, visiting shut-ins and creating inspirational booklets. I even served as elder.

Jesus said, *"It is more blessed to give than to receive."* (Acts 20:35) This was true for me. Giving of myself was healing, and I became happier. Eventually God's love led me to a life I could never have imagined possible in my early years as a Christian. Jesus gave me opportunities to serve that, at one time, would have been far beyond me.

And, I made another discovery: heirlooms made of cloth and yarn do not compare to caring for those around me. I didn't have to do anything grand. I didn't have to be famous or make a lot of money. Keeping Christ's love in my heart as I spent time with others and worked for their welfare was enough.

## I Learned to Help Others

IT IS WELL known that suffering produces compassion within a person. This has been the case for me. I feel a sisterhood with others who have mood disorders. I want to share with them the coping strategies I've discovered. It's scary to be diagnosed with bipolar disorder. As someone who has gone through it, I can encourage people as they learn to live with it simply sharing my experiences. It feels right to do this—it's what God has equipped me to do.

Reading God's word helped point me in this direction. I took to heart what Jesus said in Matthew 25: *"For I was hungry and you gave me something to eat, I was thirsty and you gave me something to drink, I was a stranger and you invited me in, I needed clothes and you clothed me, I was sick and you looked after me, I was in prison and you came to visit."* When he was asked when this had been done for him, Jesus replied, *"I tell you the truth, whatever you did for one of the least of these brothers of mine, you did for me."* I learned to understand that whatever I do for others, I do for God. And when I give to others, as I do at my *Living Room* support group, I'm no longer in the victim's role. My mental health improves.

Just as important to me as helping others cope with the symptoms of bipolar disorder is my desire to cut through the stigma that is attached to mental illness. If I could whittle away even a small part of the terrible feeling of shame that people with this disorder suffer, I would have done something meaningful.

This desire to make a difference in the lives of others with mental illness led me to become a mental health activist. It took courage to begin writing about my battles with the disease, but once my courage was in place, it never wavered. There have been times when I wandered away from that focus and followed other, more material pursuits, but I always came back, my desire to improve the lives of people with mental illness stronger than ever.

In the introduction to his book, *No Man is an Island*, Thomas Merton says that loving ourselves properly is "desiring to live, accepting life as a great gift and a great good, not because of what it gives us, but because of what it enables us to give to others." This has been true in my own life.

Although I will always have emotional struggles, I am well most of the time now. This is a great gift, and I find my greatest fulfillment in using these times of wellness to contribute to the well-being of others. I have many friends who are there for me when I need them. It's a joy to know I can be there for them as well.

# Transformed

THE CHURCH I now attend, Brentwood Park Alliance, focuses on spiritual growth. We stand back and ask ourselves whether we are the kind of presence God wants us to be in our community. We want to give to the community, not take from it. I am inspired by the way my church family consciously explores how best to serve God in the world. Through the guidance of my church, I have learned to surrender to God's leading rather than to force my own will.

I have known for many years that God loves me, but my new friends at this church have impressed this upon me. They have shown me what God's love looks like. I have grown spiritually and have undergone a transformation. I have found a greater source of strength; my courage has grown. I had always been shy about sharing my faith with others, but no longer. It's such a big part of me now that I can't help talking about it.

Shortly after joining this congregation, I began to write this book to celebrate what God has done for me. I wanted to share with other Christians what it is like to have faith in God despite suffering from a mental disorder. There is much confusion among Christians about mental health issues, and I wanted my readers to understand these issues better. Some Christians deny that these problems could have a medical cause. There is stigma within the church, just as there is among the rest of society. I wanted to focus my energy on changing this. I want to help the community of faith learn to have the compassion Jesus Christ taught.

## Letting God Lead

*"Take my life, and let it be consecrated, Lord, to Thee...Take my moments and my days...Take my hands...Take my voice...Take my will, and make it Thine; it shall be no longer mine...I will be ever, only, all for Thee."*[20]

THE WORDS OF this wonderful hymn have always meant a lot to me. Whenever I sing it, I am connected deeply with God and want to surrender my life to God in the way the words express.

Hymns such as this are one of the reasons I go to church. Church services remind me how I want God to work in my life and how I want to work for God.

I lean on God to help me in my work and my day-to-day struggles with bipolar disorder. By surrendering my will and allowing God to fill me and be with me in all I do, I have gained strength and courage. Without God, I would not be able to do what I do. I would not have begun to cry out about the injustice of stigma. I would not have found it easy to love others who suffer from bipolar disorder.

It is not by my own strength or goodness that I do God's will. My desire to follow Jesus is God-given. I can't help it. God made me for this purpose. In Philippians 2:13, Paul says, *"...for it is God who works in you to will and to act according to his good purpose."* I am the clay and God is the potter. As life goes on, God will continue to shape me. I might change, my focus might change, but by submitting to God's will, I will be the person God made me to be.

In the Message Eugene Peterson paraphrased what Jesus told his disciples in Luke 9:23–25: *"Anyone who intends to come with me has to let me lead. You're not in the driver's seat—I am. Don't run from suffering; embrace it. Follow me and I'll show you how. Self-help is no help at all. Self-sacrifice is the way, my way, to finding yourself, your true self."*

## No Longer a Victim

GOD HAS BROUGHT me a long way over the past forty years. When I think back to high school when I was withdrawn and afraid to speak in class; when I think of how sick I became and how long I stayed in hospital; when I think of how alone I was before I accepted God; I am amazed at how far I have come, at how meaningful life has become! I'm very grateful. Giving up personal willpower and placing my trust in God has given me a rich life.

Everything I do today is significant: creative activities; friendships; supporting others with mood disorders; teaching about mental illness through my writing and speaking. I feel complete. God has made me whole.

My pastor, Don, explains in a nutshell where this meaning comes from: the purpose we should have in God's great commandment is to "love God completely, and to love others compassionately and ourselves correctly."

I love God for giving me life. I love God because I can trust him to always be with me. I love God for giving me Jesus. Jesus shows me how I should live. He suffered and died for us. He is able to heal our brokenness. *"This is love: not that we loved God, but that he loved us and sent his Son as an atoning sacrifice for our sins."* (1 John 4:10)

I've found meaning in having compassion and helping others. I often look back at what Jesus said in Matthew 11:28–30: *"Come to me, all you who are weary and burdened, and I will give you rest. Take my yoke upon you and learn from me, for I am gentle and humble in heart, and you will find rest for your souls. For my yoke is easy and my burden is light."* I have found the rest Jesus spoke of, and today I carry the burden with Jesus of supporting people with mental disorders. This has given my life deep meaning.

I walk with God and let God lead. The unfolding adventure is a beautiful thing, one long mystery tour. I don't know where God will take me next, but I don't need to be afraid. *"'For I know the plans I have for you,' declares the Lord, 'plans to prosper you and not to harm you, plans to give you hope and a future.'"* (Jeremiah 29:11) My life is in God's hands.

Yes, I still have bipolar disorder, but my troubles are no longer at center stage. I am no longer a victim; I am a conqueror—a joyful one.

# AFTERWORD

*I waited patiently for the Lord; he turned to me and
    heard my cry.*
*He lifted me out of the slimy pit, out of the mud and mire;*
*he set my feet on a rock and gave me a firm place to stand.*
*He put a new song in my mouth, a hymn of praise to
    our God.*
*Many will see and fear and put their trust in the Lord.*
*(Psalm 40:1–3)*

PSALM 40 IS an encapsulation of my life. When I think back to
what I was forty-two years ago—a confused young woman in a
mental hospital—and look at what God has made me now—a
leader and activist—I am in awe. I have been transformed from a
victim of an illness into a supporter of others with illness. I am eager to tell others what God has done for me. It *is* like a miracle.

When I began writing this book, I had not thought of creating
*Living Room*, the Christian support group for people with mood
disorders. *Living Room* was born out of reflection and the writing
process. God was working in me as I poured out my thoughts and
as I was mentored, pastored and prayed for. Today the group is at
the heart of all I do.

*Living Room* has moved quickly since it was formed eighteen
months ago. The group I facilitate has forty participants, with
weekly attendance frequently over twenty. We now need to divide
into three or four smaller groups for sharing time.

I'm not alone in leading this group. Pastor Don Dyck is an ever-present support, attending meetings, ready to start us off with prayer. Janice Kellman, my right-hand help, leads the devotional when I am not able to. And the members are always willing to lend a hand: with shopping and preparing lunch, reminding others of meetings, cleaning up. Several trained co-facilitators take turns leading the small groups.

*Living Room* is not a therapy group; it is not led by professionals. Instead, it is based on self-help, facilitated by people who themselves have a mood disorder. By helping each other, we help ourselves.

An important rule at *Living Room* is "no advising, no fixing, no saving, no setting each other straight," borrowed from Parker J. Palmer's ground rules for his Quaker "circle of trust." No one has all the answers. And we don't want to make the same mistakes Job's friends made when they tried to support him in his grave illness and losses. They tried to fix Job by advising him to repent of his sin, wrongly assuming that was the problem.

Everyone at the group is fully accepted, no matter where they are emotionally or spiritually. We share openly, knowing that this is a safe place where honesty is valued and no one judges. We support each other with compassion, because we all travel similar journeys.

At *Living Room* we talk about our faith and receive prayer. We study scripture to learn how to cope with our mental health challenges. By sharing our troubles with people who understand, we find healing. At *Living Room* we can shed feelings of guilt and shame, because we no longer have to keep our mental health problems a secret.

*Living Room* has had an impact on many. "When my dad committed suicide eight months ago, it was the only place I could feel free to just talk about it. To all the other people in my life, there was shame in telling what happened." "I really believe *Living Room* has been a big part of getting me better." "If I didn't have the group, I would feel more of a freak. In the group, I am first a human being, second someone in relationship with God, and third a person with an illness. It's tangible and helps give me a healthier identity."

From the beginning, I felt that Christians everywhere needed faith-based support like this. I understood what a group like this could do for Christians with mood disorders, and I saw it as a pilot project that could serve as a model for other groups. To encourage others to form *Living Room* groups, I wrote a set of manuals describing how to set up and facilitate a group. This project was followed by a website, www.livingroomsupport.org, put together by my son, Cornelius, and his wife, Jeannette.

After a series of articles I wrote for www.canadianchristianity.com, the Christian TV program 100 Huntley Street interviewed me, and viewers from all over Canada learned about *Living Room*. The calls and e-mails flooded in. Now there are groups springing up in other communities. I wanted to help churches learn how to support people with mental health issues, and my prayers were being answered.

The *Living Room* group at my church brings me great joy. As I wrote *Riding the Roller Coaster* and this book, I could only imagine the people I was writing for—people who, like me, suffered from mood disorders. Now I can see and talk to those people, eat with them and walk with them. I can show them what God has taught me about living a tough life, and help them realize how much God loves us.

I feel the Holy Spirit at work in me as I welcome members to the meetings. Showing them God's love does not require effort. God is present in this work. I'm doing what God created me to do, and that makes me strong. After meetings I pray joyously: "Thank you, thank you, God."

# APPENDIX I

## WHAT IS BIPOLAR DISORDER?

Moods are a normal part of life. Everyone experiences ups and downs from day to day. When things are going well, the sun shines brightly on us and we feel great. But when something takes a turn for the worse—a financial problem, death in the family, loss of a job—our mood can be brought down. Even the weather can bring on misery.

For some of us, highs and lows are significantly more frequent and dramatic, to the point that they interfere with the way we normally function. This is what life is like with bipolar disorder. This disease is a mood disturbance, causing alternating and sustained periods of excessive highs (mania) and lows (depression). These mood swings can be mild, moderate or severe and will affect our thinking and behavior. Although this is a lifelong disorder, most affected people function normally between episodes. During good times, we can maintain a productive and normal lifestyle, especially when we use medication under a doctor's care.

Researchers have yet to discover the exact cause of bipolar disorder. Current evidence points to an imbalance of neurotransmitters in the brain. These are chemicals such as serotonin, norepinephrine and dopamine, which are responsible for maintaining mood levels. Scientists also know that the disorder is genetic in nature. People with a family history of the illness are more likely to develop it. As in many illnesses and disorders, stress plays a big part in triggering episodes.

# Symptoms of Bipolar Disorder

Below are symptoms of the depressed and manic phases of bipolar disorder. Other medical conditions, such as multiple sclerosis, endocrine disorders and brain tumors, can produce similar symptoms. Use of some street drugs and prescription medications, common in individuals with mental illness, can also make diagnosis difficult. If you experience the following symptoms over a period of at least two weeks, consult a doctor. It can take time to determine whether the problem is indeed bipolar disorder.

## DEPRESSION

Not all feelings of sadness or disappointment are signs of clinical depression. Only when the mood becomes pervasive and interferes with normal day-to-day functioning should you suspect depression. Five or more of the following symptoms for a period of two weeks may indicate depression:

- feeling sad, hopeless, useless, pessimistic, guilty or ashamed
- physical and mental lethargy
- loss of interest in activities that are usually enjoyed
- anxiety, worry, fear
- slowed thinking, moving and speaking
- difficulty in concentrating and making decisions
- thinking that easily becomes mixed up
- change in appetite: sometimes eating more, sometimes less
- inability to get sufficient sleep or, for some, sleeping excessively

- social withdrawal

- irritability

- crying easily or feeling a frequent need to cry

- suicidal thoughts

# MANIA

Mania is a high or elevated, expansive mood, the opposite of depression. It develops in stages, from a fairly normal, joyful state to a stronger, elated state, called "hypomania." Hypomania can move into full mania and sometimes psychosis. A person with these symptoms may find it hard to believe that he or she has [they have] a medical disorder. But if three or more of these symptoms persist to a significant degree, medical evaluation should be sought:

- euphoric, ecstatic mood

- thought processes speed up with a flood of ideas, causing rapid speech and jumping from one topic to another

- irritability and over-reacting to stimuli; sometimes becoming hostile and excessively angry over small things; also a misinterpretation of events

- rapid emotional changes: happy one minute and angry the next for no apparent reason

- inflated self-esteem, grandiosity

- excessive energy, moving from one activity to another without stopping

- going on buying sprees, incurring heavy debts and giving money away freely

- increased sex drive

- poor judgment and lack of insight—frequently a refusal to recognize that one is ill

- heightening of the senses

- psychosis: having false ideas about what is happening (delusions) or seeing or hearing things that aren't there (hallucinations)

- reduced need for sleep, sometimes only two or three hours a night

## HYPOMANIA

Hypomania is a mildly manic phase in which functioning is not usually affected to a dangerous degree. It comes with increased energy and creativity and an ability to accomplish ambitious tasks—projects that the average person would not want to try. Often there is a decreased need for sleep. Artists with bipolar disorder do some of their best work during this phase. Some people are fortunate: they have a milder form of manic depression where they experience hypomania and very little mania. For others, hypomania is a precursor to full-blown mania.

Dr. Ronald Fieve, in the epilogue of his book *Moodswing*, wrote that "people who suffer from the illness in its milder forms of moodswing tend to be magnificent performers, magnetic personalities and true achievers...Manics have not only fabulous energy when they're not too manic, but a qualitatively different, quicker, more perceptive grasp of others and of their surroundings. They are manipulators par excellence and they are also the people who get things done. Without them society would be much impoverished." It's no wonder that artists who experience hypomania will often refuse medication so that they can continue their inspired work.

## PSYCHOSIS

Psychotic symptoms are common in schizophrenia, but they can also occur in bipolar disorder if the illness is left untreated. These symptoms can include delusions, the unusual, imaginary beliefs on which patients become fixated. Delusions could be paranoia (feeling that someone is plotting against you), delusions of grandeur (exaggerated ideas of your own importance) and somatic delusions (believing you have a terminal illness). Other symptoms include hallucinations, when we see, hear, feel or smell things that are not really there. We might hear voices when no one is talking. All these thoughts and experiences seem absolutely real and are as terrifying as a nightmare.

# ELECTROCONVULSIVE THERAPY

Electroconvulsive therapy (or ECT) has had much bad press, partly because of the way it has been portrayed in movies like *One Flew Over the Cuckoo's Nest*. Seeing Jack Nicholson strapped to a table and in uncontrollable convulsions would lead anyone to think ECT was cruel and inhumane. These portrayals fail to acknowledge the benefits this therapy can provide.

At one time, there were legitimate reasons to be concerned about ECT's long-term effects. But this therapy has evolved into a safe method of helping people with severe or psychotic depression who haven't responded to medications.

The patient is put to sleep using a short-acting anesthetic, and a very small current of electricity is passed through the brain, producing a brief seizure. The seizure takes place only in the brain. The patient's body remains relaxed, with no feeling of discomfort. After ten to fifteen minutes, she wakes up. About one person in ten experiences some confusion, which clears up within twenty to sixty minutes.

How ECT works is still a bit of a mystery, but it is thought that the levels of neurotransmitters are somehow reset to a healthier level. Some patients will have short-term memory loss lasting a few days, but severe memory loss is rare with modern ECT treatments.

# APPENDIX II

# RESOURCES

## *LIVING ROOM:*
www.livingroomsupport.org
Christian support groups for people with depression, anxiety and bipolar disorders. It is an outreach program sponsored by churches, ideally in partnership with a mental health organization. As a self-help group, it is facilitated by a person who him/herself has a mood disorder. For those wishing to start up groups at their own church, help is available in the form of manuals and sample devotional materials.

## PATHWAYS TO PROMISE:
www.pathways2promise.org
An interfaith technical assistance and resource center which offers liturgical and educational materials, program models, and networking information to promote a caring ministry with people with mental illness and their families. These resources are used by people at all levels of faith group structures from local congregations to regional and national staff.

## Mental Health Ministries:
## www.mentalhealthministries.net

A ministry producing resources to educate and reduce the stigma of mental illness in faith communities. It was started by a United Methodist Minister who herself has struggled with depression but found that many clergy are not effective in providing the support and referrals that individuals and their families need.

## FaithNet NAMI:
## www.faithnet.nami.org

A network composed of members and friends of NAMI (National Alliance for the Mentally Ill). It was established for the purposes of (1) facilitating the development within the Faith Community of a non-threatening, supportive environment for those with serious mental illness and their families, (2) pointing out the value of one's spirituality in the recovery process from mental illness and the need for spiritual strength for those who are caretakers, (3) educating clergy and congregations concerning the biologic basis and characteristics of mental illness, and (4) encouraging advocacy of the Faith Community to bring about hope and help for all who are affected by mental illness.

FaithNet NAMI is not a religious network but rather an outreach to all religious organizations. It has had significant success in doing so, because all the major religions have the basic tenets of giving care and showing compassion to those in need.

# THANK YOU!

I am indebted to the many people who God has brought into my life to help me be who I am and do what I do. The following are some of those who have been important to me in recent years and to whom I am very grateful:

*Wes*, my husband, life partner and best friend. You have stood by me through my many ups and downs, always forgiving, never tiring. We've had a good marriage, haven't we?

*Helen Forewell*, my friend, mentor and sister-in-Christ. You showed me what God's love looks like. I don't think *Living Room* or this book would have happened without you.

*Don Dyck*, my pastor and friend. Your sermons have inspired me deeply. Your caring support and partnership in the undertaking of *Living Room* has helped make the group what it is. Thank you for your leadership and for not minding my endless flow of emails.

*Cita Rafferty*, my dear, ever-present friend. You're so good to talk to. I very much appreciate your desire to understand bipolar disorder.

*Diana Dyck*. Thank you for your prayers and for always having a ready ear. I especially appreciate the hugs after the *Living Room* meetings.

*Janice Kellman*. Thank you for being my right-hand at *Living Room* and helping me found our first group.

*Vicki Rogers* and *Rennie Hoffman* of the Mood Disorders Association of BC. Your help and partnership in starting a Christian support group has been invaluable. It has been good to have you walk beside us, always ready when we need encouragement or advice.

*Joyce Gram*, editor extraordinaire. You're a tough task-master, but I'm so glad you are. Knowing I had the best possible help was a comfort and encouragement. I don't know what I would have done without you.

*Cornelius Bergen* and *Jeannette Ordas*, my son and his wife. Thank you for giving so generously of your talents to my causes. I'm so fortunate to have you for my children and I'm proud of you.

*Twila Neilson*. I appreciate our friendship and enjoy our travels through the Psalms together. Thank you for your love.

*Dr. Philip Long*, my psychiatrist. Where would I be without the excellent concoction of meds you found to keep me well? Thank you for being my doctor and for encouraging me in all I do.

*Eileen Kernaghan, Julie Ferguson,* and all the members of the *Kyle Center Writer's Workshop.* You helped me write *Riding the Roller Coaster* ten years ago and now you've helped me with this book. Thank you for your inspiration and for so willingly sharing your expertise. Such a talented group you are!

My *Brentwood Park Alliance Church family.* From the time I first came a few years ago, I felt your love. In your midst I grew spiritually and was able to write this book. Thank you.

My *Living Room* group at Brentwood Park Alliance Church, an oasis of love. Meetings with you are such a delight, such a source of joy. I appreciate every one of you.

# ABOUT THE AUTHOR

Marja Bergen has been helping people who suffer from mood disorders since 1999, when her first book, *Riding the Roller Coaster* (Northstone), was published. She has counselled and supported both individuals and groups, devoting herself to reducing the stigma attached to mental illness and helping Christians learn how to be supportive. She recently established a Christian support group called *Living Room*, which was featured on the Christian television program 100 Huntley Street in January 2008.

Marja's articles, written from the perspective of a person who lives with bipolar disorder, have been published in the Vancouver Sun, Fellowship Magazine, Visions Journal, BC Christian News, Mood Disorders Association of BC newsletter, and various websites including www.canadianchristianity.com. She received a second place Fellowship of Christian Newspaper award for a First Person Article published in 2007.

Marja is an accomplished photographer, with a special interest in candid child photography. She is married to Wes and has a son, Cornelius, and daughter-in-law, Jeannette.

For more about Marja, her books and her ministry,
visit www.marjabergen.com

# NOTES

## 4. My Faith Journey

[1] Dietrich Bonhoeffer, *The Cost of Discipleship*, (SCM Press Ltd 1959), 31

## 5. Coping with the Ups and Downs

[2] Philip Yancey, *Where is God When it Hurts?* (Zondervan, 1990), 171

[3] Philip Yancey, *Soul Survivor: How my Faith Survived the Church*, (Doubleday, 2001), 218

## 6. Overcoming the Stigma

[4] Dwight L. Carlson, *Why do Christians Shoot Their Wounded? Helping (Not Hurting) Those With Emotional Difficulties*,(InterVarsity Press, 1994)

[5] *Psychiatric News* April 16, 2004; Volume 39 Number 8; Page 8

[6] Lewis L. Judd, *Decade of the Brain: Implications for Clinical Psychiatric Practice*, a lecture given at the California Psychiatric Association 1991 annual meeting, Oct 13, 1991

[7] Retrieved from moritherapy, published by GNIF Brain Blogger, an online news source on the science of mind-and-brain and the psychosocial model.

[8] Erika Bukkfalvi Hilliard, *Manic-Depressive Illness: An information booklet for patients, their families and friends*, (1997, 2nd revised edition, Dept. of Psychiatry, Royal Columbian Hospital, New Westminster, BC)

## 7. Living Day by Day

[9] Philip Yancey, *Where is God when it Hurts?* (Zondervan 1990), 31-32

## 9. Living Creatively

[10] Kay Redfield Jamison, *Touched with Fire: Manic-Depressive Illness and the Artistic Temperament,* (Free Press Paperbacks, a Division of Simon & Schuster Inc, 1993), 5

[11] D. Jablow Hershman and Julian Lieb, M.D., *The Key to Genius: Manic-Depression and the Creative Life,* (Prometheus Books, 1988), 106

[12] Ibid., 108

[13] Ronald R. Fieve, M.D., *Moodswing: Dr. Fieve on Depression,* (William Morrow and Company, Inc., 1989), 135-136

[14] Arnold M. Ludwig, The Price of Greatness: Resolving the Creativity and Madness Controversy, (The Guilford Press, 1995), 25, 157, 132

[15] Third edition of the Diagnostic and Statistical Manual of Mental Disorders (APA, 1980)

[16] Kay Redfield Jamison, *Touched with Fire: Manic-Depressive Illness and the Artistic Temperament,* (Free Press Paperbacks, A Division of Simon & Schuster Inc. 1993), 2

[17] Thomas R. Kelly, *A Testament of Devotion,* (New York: Harper & Brothers, 1941), 123-124.

[18] As quoted in *The Artist's Way: A Spiritual Path to Higher Creativity* by Julia Cameron (G.P. Putnam's Sons 1992) 4

[19] Julia Cameron, *The Artist's Way: A Spiritual Path to Higher Creativity,* (G.P. Putnam's Sons, 1992)

## 10. Finding Meaning

[20] Words by Frances R. Havergal, 1874